Heath Robinson: artist and c

Heath Robinson

Artist and comic genius
by John Lewis

Introduction by Nicolas Bentley

Constable · London

First published in Great Britain 1973
by Constable and Company Limited
10 Orange Street London WC2H 7EG
Copyright © 1973 John Noel Claude Lewis
All rights reserved
Reprinted 1973, 1982
ISBN 0 09 461600 0
Set in 11 on 12pt Monotype Baskerville
Printed in Great Britain by
St Edmundsbury Press
Bury St Edmunds, Suffolk
Designed and produced by John Lewis

Acknowledgements

Without the help of the Robinson family, I could not have written this book. My particular thanks are due to Mrs Josephine Heath Robinson and her daughter Mrs Joan Brinsmead, for their kindness, for all that they have told me and for the loan of many books and drawings; also to Oliver Robinson and Quentin Robinson for their unstinted help, particularly in reading my manuscript and suggesting various additions and alterations.

I would like to thank Lord Horder, Miss Anne James of the BBC and John Ryder of the Bodley Head for the loan of material and Michael Archer and Nicolas McDowall for the loan of books, and to acknowledge the help I have been given by David Brass and Peter Kay of the bookselling firm of E. Joseph of Charing Cross Road.

I would like to thank the following publishers, both for permission to reproduce drawings and for waiving their rights in those drawings: G. Bell and Sons Ltd, The Bodley Head, Brockhampton Press Ltd, J. M. Dent & Sons Ltd, Gerald Duckworth & Co Ltd and the Hutchinson Publishing Group Ltd.

I am most grateful to Nicolas Bentley for his encouragement and for writing his introduction to this book, and to my wife Griselda who has helped me in endless ways, and particularly in the preparation of the Bibliography and the Index.

Dedication

To Josephine Heath Robinson

Contents

List of illustrations

Colour plates

Black and white illustrations

Nicolas Bentley

Introduction

It is a rash thing to try to define humour. I am not going to take the risk, but I will go so far as to say that anyone, if such a sad creature exists, who claims to see nothing amusing in Heath Robinson's work has no means of judging the issue. Only someone without a sense of humour could fail to smile at those distortions of mechanical logic, those elaborate devices for achieving unnecessary ends, and the solemnity with which Heath Robinson's characters go about their idiotic business.

He himself was well aware of the importance of their solemnity. It is their air of earnestness and propriety, as they fiddle and fumble their way through situations of ludicrous improbability, that makes them funny. Nowadays any amateur jokesmith with a ballpoint pen can palm himself off as a humorous artist. Technique is of no account, so long as the wit is there; given a sense of the ridiculous, any competent technician can manipulate the gadgets, airbrushes, stipples, tints, the innumerable aids of Letraset, and so on, that relieve the modern draughtsman of much hard labour – and often leave their deadening imprint on his work. But in Heath Robinson's early days things were different. There were no short cuts to the effects he set out to produce. The roots of his work are in the great tradition of English comic art that first flowered with Hogarth and bloomed with Rowlandson and Gilray, then with Cruikshank, Dicky Doyle, *et al*. It was not enough that their ideas should be funny; the way they were expressed had to be amusing too, so that if you covered up the caption you would still laugh at the drawing.

Heath Robinson's early ambition was to be a landscape artist. His paintings in this genre were not commercially successful, but nor were they a waste of time. The landscape backgrounds that are significant in a good deal of his work show to what good use he put his training and experience in the difficult art of handling landscape. In this his observation was perhaps more important than either, and no doubt explains the eclecticism of his style.

If humour is difficult to define, style, as it applies to the work of an individual artist, is almost as difficult. Affinities with the work of other artists may provide a clue. Not even so idiosyncratic an artist as, say, Blake was without affinities of some sort, however obscure they may seem. There is no mystery, however, about some of the major influences in Heath Robinson's work. Among the most important that he acknowledged were Aubrey Beardsley and the now-forgotten Sidney Sime. Both are about as far removed from Hiroshige as he from Kate Greenaway, or she from Caran d'Ache, yet, as John Lewis clearly shows, each of them in their different ways influenced Heath Robinson, as did Walter Crane and the Spanish artist Daniel Vierge. In his early work, particularly in his watercolour illustrations, these influences seem more obvious than in his domestic and mechanical absurdities. In these the disparate influences of his earlier work are synthesized into a highly individual style, precise, subdued and verging on the antiquated, a style exactly suited to the grave antics of his crack-pot pragmatists, dedicated artisans, and would-be helpful members of the public.

It has always struck me as odd that an artist of such strange individuality as Heath Robinson, and of such wide popularity at the height of his career, should have had so little influence on the work of other artists. Those on whom any effect is discernible are very few. In the matter of ideas, Rowland Emmet, without directly plagiarizing those of Heath Robinson, is clearly indebted to him, and in style the niggling and erratic vibrations of Ronald Searle's line faintly echo Heath Robinson's, but influences apart from these are hard to trace. Is this perhaps because the 'intentional naïvety' that John Lewis detects in Heath Robinson's work is a quality that for some time has been out of fashion? The cult of the *faux naif* painter, assiduously fostered by some art dealers, luckily has no counterpart in illustration. The static, chic, highly stylized conventions of the 1920s which in the 1970s it became fashionable to evoke, are unsuited to expressing the sentiments of the 'philosophic clown' who, as Heath Robinson remarked in his autobiography, 'appealed to me through all my work', and of whom I suspect there was a trace in Heath Robinson himself.

If this was in fact how he saw himself as an artist – though introspection was a luxury he seemed able to do without – it is ironic that success came to him chiefly through his realistic absurdities, not through the decorative fantasies that he seemed to prefer. As time went on, the charm, the subtlety and the skill of his work in this vein became less popular, though the extraordinary variety of his advertising drawings shows how wide was the appeal of his more eccentric work. His press advertisements, booklets and brochures included illustrations for cement manufacturers, pastry-cooks, curriers, wholesale clothiers, pharmaceutical products, railways, cable drawers, process engravers and mechanical engineers, as well as other trades and business. And this in spite of the fact that he was completely ignorant about machines of any kind. John Lewis sees his working men and shop-floor mechanics as 'gentle anarchists'. I believe it was deliberately that Heath Robinson usually showed his characters bent on the surreptitious dislocation of those universal systems and devices of which the uncomprehending mass has become not a beneficiary, as was originally intended, but a helpless victim.

The curious thing about Heath Robinson's mechanisms is, as John Lewis points out apropos of an operation dependent on the property of magnetism, that 'by the laws of physics this ought not to work, but Heath Robinson makes one feel it would'. It was this topsy-turvy logic of his mechanical principles that so strongly appealed to G. K. Chesterton, who was one of his warmest admirers.

It seems to me a pity that Heath Robinson's drawings in this vein tend to overshadow the rest of his enormous output. He was a fertile, energetic and disciplined artist (unlike the impression he gave of himself in the portrait that appears on page 211), who never missed a deadline or a press date and was undaunted by the task of producing 250 illustrations for a single book, as he did for *The Arabian Nights*, or the 225 drawings which he made for an edition of Rabelais. These early works included some of the best of his coloured illustrations, which in my estimation can be ranked with those of his two contemporaries, Arthur Rackham and Edmund Dulac. But it seems that he is destined to be remembered not by works such as these, but by the freakish ingenuity of his ideas for improving the human lot and by those staid, grotesque 'sad-eyed victims of circumstances', as John Lewis aptly describes them, by whom his weird world was populated.

John Lewis's resuscitation of much of Heath Robinson's early work and his assessment of his position in the hierarchy of English book illustrators and comic draughtsmen is more than a well-deserved tribute to a unique artist. It is a work of patient research, keen observation and objective judgement that must be regarded as the definitive account of Heath Robinson's career and achievement.

Grand-father Robinson at work engraving a wood block. This is after a sketch made by Will's uncle, Charles Robinson. From *My Line of Life*, published by Blackie & Sons. 1938.

Chapter One

His life and background

William Heath Robinson was a book illustrator of great distinction and he was a humorous draughtsman of genius. He was also not the kind of man who would have thought he merited a biography, though I feel he might have been touched to find that over a quarter of a century after his death, someone was prepared to discuss his work seriously – and particularly what he called his 'serious work'.

In this chapter to give some substance to what follows, I have traced the main events of his life and given something of his background and perhaps an indication of the kind of man he was.

His story was a plain uneventful tale of a very talented artist who soon found his métier, was happily married and was never to be out of work. This is not to say that the Robinsons were wealthy people. Illustration has never been a road to riches. Every penny that the free-lance artist earns has to be made as a result of the labour of his own hands. This means a lot of very hard work to make even a reasonable living, and if he is in bed with a cold he earns nothing. As Mrs Heath Robinson recently and rather ruefully remarked, 'He was not in the least interested in money'.

In the 1930s at the height of his fame as a comic draughtsman, when he was working for the weekly magazines such as *The Sketch* and *The Bystander*, the most he ever received for one of his full-page drawings was about 15 guineas. This probably involved a week's work, and in the case of advertising drawings, the preparation of rough sketches as well. In later life he was sometimes a little saddened that he had spent far more time on comic drawings than on illustrating books, but he put just as much care and thought into his comic drawings, for he was a professional in a family of professional artists.

Heath Robinson's grandfather, Thomas Robinson, was a Northumberland man who began his working life as a bookbinder in Newcastle-upon-Tyne and on occasions worked for the great Thomas Bewick. He also bound books for George Stephenson, the builder of some of the first steam locomotives. He knew Stephenson personally. For reasons unknown to his grandson, Thomas Robinson decided to make for London, just as Thomas and John Bewick did. Like the Bewicks, he took the cheapest route, a passage in a Newcastle collier brig, bound with a cargo of seacoals for London River.

Unlike Thomas Bewick, who quickly returned to Newcastle, Thomas Robinson settled in London. He must have been a man of varied talents, for he gave up his bookbinding trade to become a wood engraver. With the great increase in a literate public, illustrated magazines, journals and books proliferated so the reproduction wood engraver was in great demand. Thomas Robinson engraved blocks for *Good Words*, *The London Journal* and other magazines, from the drawings of George du Maurier and many other artists, including Sir John Gilbert who was to influence the early work of his grandson, William Heath Robinson.

Heath Robinson's grandfather, on his mother's side, was an innkeeper named William Heath who was the landlord of various public houses including one at Hammersmith. The only things he bequeathed to his grandson were his names.

Heath Robinson's father was also called Thomas Robinson. As a boy he had been apprenticed to a watchmaker. Later he forsook this trade and took up wood engraving, finally relinquishing this burdensome work to become an illustrator in his own right.

Thomas Robinson became the chief staff artist to the *Penny Illustrated*. For many years he drew the front-page illustration for this popular journal. His subjects were sometimes of past happenings, which were lifted from old numbers of *The Illustrated London News*, but more often were of contemporary events. The Tay Bridge disaster which happened on the night of 28 December 1879 was one event for which he did a lively drawing. Another and typical Thomas Robinson illustration, published on 8 May 1880, was a vivid engraving of a 'Fatal Fire in Aldersgate Street', which was sub-headed 'A warning to the City of London'.

The Penny Illustrated, first published in 1861, was edited by John Latey, the son of John Lash Latey, the editor for fifty years of *The Illustrated London News*. John Latey Jr left *The Penny Illustrated* to become the first editor of *The Sketch*. He had a pretty daughter called Josephine who was to become Heath Robinson's wife. The Robinsons were a tightly knit family. Thomas's only brother Charles was employed on work similar to his brother's by *The Illustrated London News*. The two brothers were the closest of friends. Thomas had six children. The three eldest of the younger generation of Robinsons, Tom, Charles and William Heath were just as attached to each other as had been their father and his brother.

William Heath Robinson was born at Hornsey Rise in North London on 31 May 1872. He had a happy childhood in which home meant more to him than the schools he attended. He and his brothers had few toys so they had to rely on their imagination for their entertainment. The boys would spend hours drawing on their slates telling stories of pirates and highwaymen in this manner, and modifying the drawings by sponge and slate pencil as the stories progressed.

The Robinson family usually spent their summer holidays at Ramsgate. The drawings that Will was to do in later years of flat sands and far receding tides must have dated from the impressions received on the walks that he and his brothers took along the shores of Pegwell Bay. In winter they had one great event to look forward to and that was the Christmas Pantomime at the Standard Theatre at Hoxton, or the Eagle in City Road. They

'The Tay Bridge Disaster', 28 December 1879, engraved by Thomas Robinson for the front cover of *The Penny Illustrated Paper*.

always hoped it would be at the Standard Theatre for this meant that they would have to stay a night with some relations who kept a public house in Whitechapel. After the theatre, they would be taken back to the inn in a four-wheeled cab and led upstairs to bed through the private bar with its blaze of lights, brilliant cut-glass partitions, polished mahogany counters, stout pink-and-white bar maids and a genial and warm alcoholic atmosphere.

In 1887, when Heath Robinson was fifteen, he left school. He had only one ambition and that was to be an artist like his father and his two brothers, for Tom and Charles had already started on careers in art: Tom as a student at the Islington Art School as a preliminary to entering the Royal Academy Schools, and Charles as an apprentice lithographer. Will also became a student at the art school at Islington. Writing about this moment in a young artist's life, he said: 'Frankly there was no limit to my ambition. Not that I told myself I should rival Velasquez or Rembrandt, but there was at that stage of my artistic career a pleasing indefiniteness as to my future development. To me, as yet, anything seemed possible. I flattered myself with the possibilities rather than the probabilities of what was waiting for me in the future.'[1]

The drabness of the antique room at the art school hardly matched the young Heath Robinson's artistic flights of fancy. He said: 'We lived in a world of plaster of Paris, the studio was crowded with the Discobolus, busts of Roman emperors and empresses, the Venus of Medici, the head and shoulders of the Hermes of Praxiteles and fragments of many other well known examples of the plastic arts. We became so accustomed to drawing fragments, that we were inclined to prefer figures in a state of mutilation to the commonplace examples with the normal number of limbs.'[2]

To gain admission to the Royal Academy Schools, students had to prepare a certain number of drawings from the actual examples of Greek and Roman sculpture, rather than the dusty, debased plaster of Paris copies that cluttered up every school of art in those perhaps less enlightened days. Heath Robinson said about this '. . . we now entered upon the marble state of our art education and glutted ourselves with the antique'.

At his second attempt he gained entry to the R.A. Schools, only to find to his dismay that after five years of drawing from the antique, he was still expected to continue this boring task. However, there was the compensation of a certain amount of drawing and painting in the life class. Among his contemporaries at the R.A. Schools were Charles Sims, G. E. Stampa and Lewis Baumer (both later to become regular contributors to *Punch*),

[1] W. Heath Robinson, *My Line of Life*, London, Blackie & Son Ltd, 1938.

[2] Ibid.

'Fatal fire in Aldersgate Street: a Warning to the City of London', engraved by Thomas Robinson for the front cover of the 8 May 1880 number of *The Penny Illustrated Paper*.

Silhouettes cut by Thomas Robinson of his wife and her younger sister and brother.

Byam Shaw and F. O. Salisbury who in his turn earned wealth and fame as a painter of coronations and other stately occasions.

It is not at all clear how much or how little time Heath Robinson spent at the Royal Academy Schools. He himself wrote that his attendance at the Schools was never very regular. According to Josephine Heath Robinson, he left there before he should have done. She said: 'I think he was there for rather less than three years.' The need to support himself was pressing and he soon brought his academic career to a close.

He then set out on the improbable course of earning his living as a landscape painter. As Greece, Rome or the Himalayas were a bit out of reach, for one beautiful summer, he settled on Hampstead Heath and Highgate Ponds for his painting grounds in the company of a few other eccentrics. At the end of the summer he sold just one painting to the mother of a friend, who no doubt bought it out of kindness. On the strength of this, he and his friend went off to Cornwall for a short holiday. They stayed in a little stone cottage at Lelant, near St Ives. The memory and the glamour of what he called 'that light-drenched land' remained with him all his life.

One picture bought out of kindness did not seem, to the young Will Heath Robinson, to be sufficient grounds for establishing a career. Both his brothers, following in their father's wake, were selling drawings to magazines. Will, without too many pangs, gave up the idea of becoming another Constable or Turner, and with a desk in the corner of his father's studio at No 1 Danes Inn, in the Strand, he began work on a portfolio of illustrations that he could hawk round the publishing houses. He writes about this decision: 'Ever since the days when we amused ourselves with drawing on slates, we had been in the habit of filling sketch books with slight drawings prompted by fancy or imagination . . . I believe this habit played a greater part in our artistic careers than the more academic training we received at our art schools.'[1] The sketch books that have survived are full of drawings of his family and his cats. Often they were very slight scribbles, though in one book there are some striking portrait heads, as well as studies of costume, animals, birds, leaves and flowers.

Danes Inn must have been a dreary place after Hampstead Heath. Flights of stairs with iron railings led to Thomas's studio on the top floor. Heath Robinson remarked on the fact that the only thing that belied its prison-like character was a smell of old dinners. In his father's studio, the smell of cabbage and mutton chops gave way to a dusty, nose-tickling sensation. The dried body of a cat was nailed up near the fireplace – an unlikely object for a family of cat lovers. A large allegorical print representing 'The Spirit of Gout' hung on one of the walls. Tom and Charles were

[1] *My Line of Life.*

already working there and none of them seems to have been unduly upset by this Dickensian setting.

When he had completed enough drawings to make some sort of showing, Heath Robinson set out with his portfolio. He made the rounds of the publishing houses, with the usual lack of success. However, he eventually sold some illustrations to *Good Words* and a drawing to Cassells for *Little Folks*. This was the beginning. Soon work was coming to him, saving the young artist the wearisome business of presenting himself with his portfolio to publishers, just as if he was some hawker selling bootlaces or clothes' pegs.

The studio at Danes Inn had become too confining so with an artist friend called P. J. Billinghurst, Heath Robinson took a studio which had been built over a stable in Howland Street, off Tottenham Court Road. His German-Jewish landlady's name was Schmidt, a name familiar in that neighbourhood. On some days the presence of the stable made itself felt, not only by the stamping of the dray horses in their stalls, but by an overpowering ammoniacal stench, that could almost be seen as it rose through the cracked floorboards.

A few months of this was more than enough for Heath Robinson and Percy Billinghurst. They found a flimsy wooden structure built on the top of a house in Gower Street. The stable smells were now replaced by draughts from every point on the compass. They often felt they might be blown off the roof. If this had happened they had hopes that they would land on the top of the premises of one of the publishers, such as Dent's, Bell's or David Nutt's, and literally take them by storm. The year was 1896, Heath Robinson was twenty-four and beginning to be independent of family help.

On his rounds of the book publishers, Heath Robinson had visited John Lane in his pretty little house in Vigo Street and Dent and Heinemann in Bedford Street, both within smelling distance of Covent Garden vegetable market. He had called on Grant Richards, who in January 1897 had set up as a publisher in Leicester Square; also on David Nutt, a scholar bookseller in the Strand; lastly on the firm of Bliss, Sands and Co. To begin with, all he got out of this was a venerable blessing from the venerable Mr Dent, but this was something, for had not Mr Dent given young Beardsley his first commission?

In 1897, Will Heath Robinson received *his* first commission to illustrate a book from Bliss, Sands. His visits to the publishers had not been without profit. This was progress and Heath Robinson was now almost out of his apprenticeship. Publishers were coming to have faith in the youngest of the three Robinson brothers. Tom and Charles were both well established: among other work Tom had illustrated Sterne's *A Sentimental Journey* and

'King Lear'. Drawing by Sir John Gilbert from Staunton's *Shakespeare's Works*. 1856–58.
Thomas Robinson engraved many of Gilbert's drawings and Gilbert was one of the first
artists to influence Heath Robinson's work.

'You are in the cavern of the winds'. Illustration by T. H. Robinson for 'The Garden of Paradise' from the 1899 *Hans Andersen*, published by J. M. Dent and Sons Ltd. All three Robinson brothers collaborated in the illustrations of this edition.

Away she danced, and away she had to dance, right away into the Dark Forest

'Away she danced'. Illustration by Charles Robinson for 'The Red Shoes' from the 1899 *Hans Andersen*, published by J. M. Dent and Sons Ltd.

'Hans Clodhopper astride his billy-goat'. Illustration by W. Heath Robinson from the 1899 edition of Hans Andersen's *Fairy Tales*. Published by J. M. Dent and Sons Ltd.

was at this time working on drawings for an edition of *Cranford*. Both these books were for Bliss, Sands and Co. Charles had achieved even more fame with his illustrations for Robert Louis Stevenson's *A Child's Garden of Verses*, which Lane had published in 1896.

As well as the four Robinson boys, there were two girls, Mary, who was next in line to Will, and Florence who was the youngest. Mary became a most distinguished scribe and illuminator and exhibited on many occasions at exhibitions arranged by the Society of Scribes and Illuminators. Florence (Aunty Lolly as the young Heath Robinsons called her) was a talented artist. She married but continued to paint throughout her life.

In *My Line of Life*, Heath Robinson gives an amusing description of Sundays at the Robinson home: 'However much we wandered during the week, on Sunday we found a common meeting place at home. The Sunday mid-day dinner was still my mother's achievement of the week. It was a work of art, a symphony in roast beef, baked potatoes and puddings.' After this gastronomic concert had been digested, the young men departed to collect their future brides, glorious in leg-of-mutton sleeves and flounced skirts, to bring them home to tea. After tea they would gather round the piano 'for the Robinsons were incorrigible singers'.

When Will was doing his Sunday courting of Josephine, he always attended at her home dressed in a frock coat, pepper and salt trousers and a top hat. 'It was the normal dress for people of our class in those days,' Josephine remarked. 'Throughout his life he always wore a stiff collar. When I first knew him it was about three inches high, but in later life it dwindled to less choking proportions.'

Will, as a young man, was a spare figure with a mop of brown hair and hazel eyes (no glasses, he only wore them for work), a pale complexion and a large moustache. From early days he favoured tweed suits with rather discreet chequerboard patterns. On more formal occasions, he was always in navy blue or dark grey.

The Boer War was nearing its end, the disasters and joys of this sad conflict were sharply focused by Rudyard Kipling's patriotic verse. In 1902, Heath Robinson's father died, followed only a few months later by Josephine's father, John Latey.

Heath Robinson's circle of friends was widening. He had joined the London Sketch Club, which in those days used to meet in an old studio on the ground floor of a house in Marylebone Road. This studio was a room of considerable character, dilapidated but full of pictures, old coke stoves, scrubbed tables and tobacco smoke. The Club whose members were mainly illustrators and cartoonists, met on Friday evenings during the winter. There was usually a model available. After the drawing session was over they would sit down to drink and to eat a 'very substantial dinner'. The evening would finish with music and various other entertainments. When Heath Robinson joined the London Sketch Club, Bert Thomas was already a member as were H. M. Bateman, Edmund Dulac, Dudley Hardy, John Hassall and Frank Reynolds. It proved a happy meeting ground even for one as reserved as Heath Robinson.

As well as these solid, flesh-and-blood friends, there was an imaginary character called Uncle Lubin, whom Heath Robinson described as his 'good genius'. In fact in *My Line of Life*, he devotes a chapter to him.

This odd conception is worth some attention. Among the illustrations for *The Adventures of Uncle Lubin* were the forerunners of all those drawings of complicated, ramshackle contraptions that at some point or other depend so heavily on knotted pieces of string. For the last sixty to seventy years, such contraptions have been known by the term 'Heath Robinson'. It was about the turn of the century that William Heath Robinson says he was conscious of being haunted by this strange little character.

Uncle Lubin's origins were obscure, though Heath Robinson said 'He must have wandered long in Alice's Wonderland . . . he was sincerity itself and he had the simplicity of a child and the wisdom of Old Father William. No mortal could compare with him for ingenuity or inventiveness. He could do wonderful things with pieces of string. There was one thing that he lacked and that was a sense of humour. Perhaps this was not a loss *for strangely enough it made him all the more humorous*.'[1] And here, neatly put, is the secret of W. Heath Robinson's comic drawings. The solemnity of the little men drilling holes in Gruyère cheese or testing artificial teeth with what looks like pile-driving equipment make their ludicrous activities all the more believable, and all the funnier for that.

By 1903 Josephine Latey and William Heath Robinson had been engaged for four and half years. They felt that this was about long enough. Both Tom and Charles were married, but it was not until *Uncle Lubin* was published that they felt they could afford to get married. At about this time Heath Robinson was approached by a Canadian businessman from Toronto who signed himself Chas. E. Potter, with a proposal that he should do some commercial work, in fact a series of drawings for advertisements for the Lamson Paragon Supply Company.

The photograph of Will's and Josephine's wedding group seems rather more cheerful than those kind of gatherings usually are. In the centre of the picture the pretty bride sits, dressed in a pearl grey dress with a frilled skirt and a large and beautiful hat with trailing ribbons. She is holding an

[1] *My Line of Life.* The italics are mine not H.R.'s. J.L.

Sketch Club portrait from one of Heath Robinson's sketch books.

ornate bouquet. The reason she was not dressed in white with a veil and all the rest of it was that as her father had only died six months earlier, her mother felt that some attempt at mourning should be made. Will stands behind his bride, distinguished by a luxuriant moustache. His three brothers stand near him. The men are all dressed in frock coats.

After the wedding ceremonies were over it started to rain. They departed by cab for Waterloo station and took the train to Bournemouth, a sober resort on the South Coast. They fondly hoped that no one would recognize them as newly weds.

Their first home was a very small furnished flat up many flights of stone stairs on the top floor of a building next door to a music-hall, the Holloway Empire.

Soon after their marriage, Heath Robinson had the unpleasant experience of having to go to court as a creditor in a bankruptcy case. This was to do with the non-payment for some drawings. The bankrupt was Grant Richards, the publisher of *Uncle Lubin*. Heath Robinson did not get his money and found the majesty of the law somewhat alarming. If they had known how unstable Grant Richards' publishing house was, they might even have had second thoughts about matrimony, but Chas. E. Potter's proposition proved to be a more profitable undertaking.

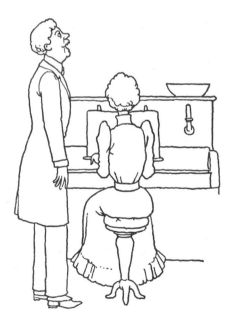

'The Robinsons were incorrigible singers'.

Heath Robinson had always found the job of dealing with clients, seeking work and fighting for better terms altogether irksome, and on the advice of a friend, he placed himself in the hands of an Artist's Agent called A. E. Johnson. They had a long and happy relationship – to the lasting benefit of both sides, though Johnson was better at finding fresh outlets for Heath Robinson's work than he was at getting good terms for his artist. Later on Johnson's firm was joined by the brothers Ernest and Sydney Boot. From 1919 onwards Sydney Boot took over the responsibility of handling all Heath Robinson's transactions.

Work was now coming in with fair regularity. In 1903–4 his illustrations ranged from some comic coloured drawings for a book called *The Monarchs of Merry England* to his remarkable set of black-and-white illustrations for *Rabelais*.

The Heath Robinsons soon left their furnished flat and the distant sounds of applause from the music-hall next door for a more comfortable apartment, in which they could have their own furniture. This was in Cathcart Hill, Junction Road, and here in 1904, their first child Joan was born. Heath Robinson was now working in an attic studio in New Court, Carey Street, in the same building as his brothers. He shared this with a rather pathetic Eurasian friend called E. Cockburn Reynolds, who shortly afterwards expired from tuberculosis.

In 1908, the Heath Robinsons' eldest son, Oliver, was born. The Cathcart Hill flat now began to feel a bit confining, so in the following year they emigrated to Hatch End, Pinner, in what was then still a relatively rural Middlesex. They rented a little villa, one of a small colony of similar houses, set in the midst of open country. Here there was room for Heath Robinson to work, so he gave up his studio in New Court. From this time onwards, he always worked at home, though when they moved to Cranleigh, he built a studio in the garden, probably as a refuge from his growing family.

Bert Thomas, the *Punch* artist and a London Sketch Club acquaintance, came to live at Pinner at much the same time as the Robinsons. They soon became firm and lasting friends.

Heath Robinson was now spending more time on his comic drawings than he was on his serious illustration. His comic series of absurdities and inventions were appearing weekly in *The Sketch* and other papers and his name was already becoming a household word. According to Langston Day,[1] it was certainly in use some years before the First World War, when in the House of Commons a member who had just returned from an air display in Austria referred to the aircraft as 'Heath Robinson contraptions'.

[1] Langston Day, *The Life and Art of W. Heath Robinson*, Herbert Joseph, London, 1947.

In 1909, their second son Alan was born and in 1912 a third son Quentin arrived. His growing family was the inspiration for Heath Robinson to write and draw the adventures of *Bill the Minder*. Life in Hatch End and in the days before the First World War seemed to be happy for the Robinson family.

When his daughter Joan was still quite a little girl, she invited two of her friends to tea. They entered the dining room to find Will seated in an arm-chair with a flower pot doing duty as a hat. The little girls did not know whether he was being funny or not, so they did not dare to smile. Neither did Will, so they all had a very solemn tea and the flower pot remained in position.

One of his great pleasures was to take his children for long walks and teach them to use their eyes. Joan remembers being asked the colour of the shady side of a haystack.

'Yellow, of course,' she said.

'It's not,' her father replied, 'Look again.' She did, and finally came up with the right answer of blue and mauve.

'He was most encouraging,' she said. 'We were always allowed into his studio to draw and to use his paints and brushes. He was the kindest man – and the stories he used to tell us! He used to make up wonderful tales, which he told in serial form. One bit one day and one the next and so on.'

In the evenings, Will and his brother Tom would foregather in the snug little bar of the Queen's Head. Here with the village worthies they would discuss the affairs of the world (or of Pinner) with that solemnity given by a pint or two of old-and-mild. At the time of the annual fair, the taproom would be packed out with showmen and the rest of that unknown world of gipsy fortune-tellers, coconut-shy men and roundabout proprietors.

Will and Tom and one or two friends used to take long walks through the Middlesex countryside. Once it was a midnight walk. They caught the last train to Chorley Wood and set out to walk through the night to Den-ham and then back home again. It was a lovely July night with a full moon and the woods seemed as if they were filled with magic. Will said: 'We had not the luck of Bottom, Snout or Starveling. We saw neither Oberon nor Titania.'[1] Yet he communicated something of the magic of that night when in the following year he illustrated *A Midsummer Night's Dream* for Constable.

These walks became a regular feature in their life. So much so that they formed a walking club, which they called 'The Frothfinders Federation'. The Robinson brothers of course were members, as were various artist friends. Their walks as often as not ended in a pub. At the very end of his autobiography, Heath Robinson said: 'I may not have romped in the

[1] *My Line of Life.*

woods of Arcady, but I have had some pleasant evenings in the Crown at Stanmore'.

On one occasion the three brothers took part in a Special Frothfinder's Night's Entertainment, which was held at a pub. Tom who was the smallest of the three elder brothers played the part of a baby, dressed in a nightgown with a dummy in his mouth. Charles was a nurse, and brought on the 'baby' in a wheelbarrow, doing duty for a pram. Most surprising of all, Will took the part of a fairy, dressed in a tutu, a wig and pink tights. Two large sugar basins were strapped to his thin chest to provide him with appropriate statistics. Josephine, to her intense annoyance, was not allowed to attend. When she remonstrated with Will, he said: 'I don't think it would be at all a suitable exhibition for you to see!'

Will has described how after the Frothfinders Federation walks, they would eat an enormous meal at the Crown Inn and then rouse the neighbourhood with their songs. He wrote: 'There must be something pagan in me, for whom these choruses had an almost religious sublimity. . . . For a few minutes you are completely at one with each other. The chorus ends and you are individuals again. But perhaps as the reader may have observed, I am a sentimental man.'[1]

On August Bank Holiday in 1914, after another of their walks, the Robinson brothers were tramping home in the dusk. They heard in the distance the sound of hoof beats and shortly afterwards a cavalry orderly galloped past them, leading an officer's remount. He seemed to them to be an outrider of war, a symbol of the coming conflict.

Heath Robinson had recently finished his beautiful set of drawings for the *Dream* and was beginning work on *The Water Babies*. Now there was little demand for such work, everything had to be slanted to the war effort. However, the much-vaunted prowess and efficiency of the German armed forces provided him with a perfect subject for his humour. His drawings were appearing in *The Sketch* and *The Bystander* and were later to be republished as books under the titles of *Some Frightful War Pictures*, *Hunlikely* and *The Saintly Hun*. They were the most deflating, pomposity-pricking pieces of propaganda and enheartened many an officer's mess or dug-out in Flanders. Heath Robinson and Bruce Bairnsfather were the two British comic artists of the 1914–18 war who did most to relieve the gloom of those fearful years.

For most of the war, the Heath Robinsons lived in Pinner, though they moved to a house nearer the village. They were within sound of the air raids. In a letter to a friend written on 30 July 1917, Heath Robinson wrote: 'We hear the guns etc., very plainly from here and see the shrapnel

[1] Ibid.

Costume studies from one of Heath Robinson's sketch books, possibly for *Twelfth Night*.

'The Rick'. Watercolour drawing by William Heath Robinson.

bursting in the sky. Pinner, however, seems quite a safe place . . . during the summer we became a sort of spa or watering place; many people not caring to go further afield for their holidays.'[1]

Later on in the war, Heath Robinson was commissioned to make humorous drawings of the United States Army in France. To this end, he visited France and was arrested for sketching the harbour at St Nazaire. After his release from that predicament, he moved to the American front in Lorraine. Here he met Louis Raemakers, the great Belgian cartoonist, for whom he had the deepest admiration.

During the war, the only important pieces of book illustration that Heath Robinson carried out were for Charles Kingsley's *The Water Babies* which was one of the most successful things he ever did, and for Walter de la Mare's *Peacock Pie*. Both these books suffered in the quality of their production from war-time economies.

In March 1918, the Robinsons moved from Pinner to Cranleigh. One of the reasons for this was the need to educate their still growing family. Early in the following year the youngest boy Tom was born. Oliver went as a day boy to Cranleigh, to be followed in due course by the three other boys, and Joan was sent to St Catherine's at Bramley. Cranleigh proved a happy place in which the Robinsons could grow up, but maybe wherever Will and Josephine Heath Robinson lived would have become a happy place. They soon made many friends in a neighbourhood of mainly retired army or professional men. Yet as Will observed: 'One advantage that an artist has over others lies in the fact that he does not belong to any particular class. Class distinctions do not exist for him to the same extent as they do for other people.'[2]

When working in the garden he was in the habit of wearing the most dreadful old clothes and because of this was more than once mistaken for the gardener. On one occasion an artist dressed in a pale violet-grey suit, with a black velvet collar, called on the Robinsons. He saw Will digging in the garden and shouted across to him: 'Is your master in, my man?' 'I'll go and see,' muttered Will and disappeared indoors, only to appear a moment later in a tidier jacket and with his hair brushed, to make himself known to the other artist. What the outcome of this was, I do not know. In his autobiography he tells this tale and gives the unnamed visitor the soubriquet of Renée de Boudoir.

In middle age, though Heath Robinson's hair had thinned and his moustache had turned grey, his looks had not changed much. The pince-nez that he wore when working had been replaced by circular shell-

[1] *My Line of Life.*

[2] Ibid.

'Artists seldom retire', from Heath Robinson's autobiography, published in 1938.

rimmed glasses. His tweed suits still tended to formality and he remained faithful to a trilby hat.

There was a leavening of artists in Cranleigh. Edmund Dulac, illustrator, and Bertram Prance, the *Punch* artist, lived nearby. Alfred Leete (the artist who drew that awesome poster of Kitchener pointing his accusing finger) had a son at the school and was a frequent visitor, as was Bert Thomas, whose eldest boy was also at the school; and H. M. Bateman used to drive over from his house at Reigate to visit the Robinsons. Lawson Wood, animal caricaturist, lived near the Robinsons. When he left the neighbourhood, Frank Swinnerton, the novelist, took his cottage.

In 1920, Heath Robinson provided two selections of his drawings for his brother George to publish. George was the only one of the Robinson brothers who was not an artist. He had tried various jobs and was at this time setting up as a publisher. He was the youngest of the brothers. Quentin Robinson remembers his uncle as a man of great charm, whom the children adored. This may have been because he used to conspire with them against parental authority. His frequent change of jobs resulted from his refusal to make any concessions to the views of his employers if he thought them wrong. Several times in his career he started as a travelling representative. By his aptitude and hard work, he quickly rose to a high managerial position, only to quarrel with his bosses, throw the job in and start all over again with some other firm. His only real failure, sad to say, was his publishing venture. There must have been more than a little of the artist in George.

Of the two books of drawings that George Robinson published, one was called *Get On With It* and the other *Quaint and Selected Pictures*. They were inexpensively produced with paper covers. Whether they even recovered their printing costs is not recorded.

While the Robinsons were living at Cranleigh, Will devoted much of his studio time to water-colour painting, working largely from his imagination. Throughout his career, he kept this side of his work to the fore and also, whenever possible he would go out into the Surrey fields and woodlands, as he said, 'to indulge in my old love of landscape painting'. This helped to keep his vision fresh. It was like recharging the batteries.

The Robinsons lived at Cranleigh from 1918 to 1929. Then, when the two eldest boys had left school, they decided to move back to London to provide a home for them. While Heath Robinson was at Cranleigh, he continued to pour out his comic inventions for the weekly magazines and did more and more drawings for advertising purposes.

Sometimes Will would call Josephine or one of the children into the studio to see if they could see the point of one of his funny drawings. 'He used to get very irritable with me if I could not see immediately how some of his most complicated machines worked', Josephine said.

In the summer, the family had holidays at Bognor and other South Coast resorts. Once they visited Waxham in Norfolk and later, when the children were grown up, Will and Josephine had a memorable holiday at Holkham. He loved the clear East Anglian light and did many sketches of Blakeney and the surrounding country.

During their time at Cranleigh, as well as all his comic work, Heath Robinson had illustrated *Old Time Stories* by Perrault which had been translated from the French by his old friend and agent A. E. Johnson. This attractive book, published in 1921 by Constable, was one of the last serious pieces of illustration that he undertook.

The future well-being of his family was to depend on his comic absurdities in the weekly magazines and the equally comic drawings that were commissioned by industry and commerce. They must have presented real problems. He wrote that: 'When first of all confronted with such formidable operations as the rolling out of white-hot steel bars, the manufacture of cement, or the hammering out of steel plates, I despaired of drawing the slightest spark of humour from them.'[1] He extracted plenty of fun from these and even more unpromising subjects, and by the seriousness with which he tackled his absurd solutions to his customers' processes and problems made them all the funnier.

By the 1920s William Heath Robinson was a famous man. His fame was not due to his fine book illustrations but to the absurdities and inventions that appeared week after week in *The Sketch*, *The Bystander* and other journals. The side-effects of his reputation as a great comic artist were varied and various. In 1923 the BBC invited him to broadcast from Savoy Hill. This was the first of several radio appearances. In 1930 he decorated an Atlantic liner – at least, he decorated the Knickerbocker Bar and the Children's Room in the *Empress of Britain*. In 1934, he designed a house for the *Daily Mail* Ideal Home Exhibition, and in 1938 the BBC televised Heath Robinson and his Pea Splitting Machine. These activities no doubt gave great satisfaction to his agent and his commercial customers. To Will himself they were a doubtful pleasure. He was not one who enjoyed being lionized.

In his normal daily life his pattern of working was absolutely constant. After breakfast he took the previous day's work off to the post and went for a walk. When he returned to the house, he would pick up one of his beloved cats (at Highgate it was a ginger-and-white Tom called Saturday Morning) and go off to his studio. Often he would work until ten or eleven at night. Apart from this pattern of working he was not particularly methodical, but he was most punctilious about keeping delivery dates for his work.

* *My Line of Life.*

In 1929, the Heath Robinsons settled down in Highgate, first in Shepherd's Hill and later in a house in Southwood Avenue. Will was now once again able to enjoy his Friday evenings at the London Sketch Club and to visit the Savage Club which was then in Adelphi Terrace. He had been a member of the Savage Club for some years and here he met once again many old friends from earlier days at the London Sketch Club, including the black-and-white artists Bert Thomas, George L. Stampa and George Belcher, all of whom worked for *Punch;* and Tom Purvis the poster artist. Here he also met the political cartoonist David Low and Percy V. Bradshaw, who ran a successful correspondence school for would-be illustrators. Heath Robinson had provided the material for part of one of Bradshaw's illustration courses.

At home, if he was not drawing, he was reading. His favourite authors were Charles Dickens, Thomas Hardy and the great Russian novelists. He was particularly fond of Dickens. Despite the curious mechanical bent of his comic inventions, Heath Robinson was no mechanic and, according to his wife, was quite useless with his hands.

As William Heath Robinson grew older, he visited his club less and less often. He liked to potter about at home, or to walk in Waterlow Park, Highgate, from where he could see distant views of St Paul's Cathedral and where old men would gather on park benches and argue just as if they were sitting in deep armchairs at the Savage Club or the Athenaeum. He liked to watch what he termed 'ordinary people', children dancing in the sunlight, old ladies mumbling their sandwiches, lovers holding hands. He felt happy and at one with them, for in his extreme modesty, he felt he was a very ordinary person.

As a man, he was shy and withdrawn. When I asked his eldest son, Oliver, 'Were you close to him?', he replied, 'He was not the kind of man you could be close to. We were much nearer to him when we were little children. He felt happy with the very young, but not with sons who were growing up.'

Quentin agreed with his brother's observation, but said that after living at home for three years, just before the last war, he began to get to know his father for the first time on level terms. 'I found him an interesting amalgam of a free-thinker who really longed to be a convinced believer, and an extremely broad-minded man who could yet be astonishingly prudish. About art of any kind, the keynote of his position was that however adventurous it might be, it must have a foundation in technical proficiency. He used to say of Picasso that he did not understand much of his work, but he was prepared to respect it because he had proved he could draw.' The last observation is revealing, for in those days the name of Picasso was absolute anathema to most academic artists.

William Heath Robinson and his ginger-and-white cat Saturday Morning.

In the last year of his life, he did little work, in the last nine months when he was ill, practically none at all.

When he was very near his end, he said to his wife Josephine: 'I am afraid I have not left you much, but perhaps one day, my work may mean something to somebody....'

On 13 September 1944 William Heath Robinson, artist and comic genius, died, aged 72 years.

'Or to walk in Waterlow Park, Highgate', from *My Line of Life*.

Chapter Two

His development as an illustrator

William Heath Robinson began work in the 1890s. Today, three-quarters of a century away, there is a tendency to view this period through the eyes of Toulouse-Lautrec and Beardsley. We see Paris through the smoke-laden atmosphere of the Moulin Rouge. We think of a London of pea-soup fogs, hansom cabs, Sherlock Holmes, Oscar Wilde, the shocking yellow of *The Yellow Book*, but above all of Aubrey Beardsley.

Aubrey Beardsley, who was born in the same year as William Heath Robinson, had only six crowded years of productive work. His first book illustrations for *Le Morte d'Arthur* were published by J. M. Dent in 1893, his last for *Mademoiselle de Maupin* were published by Leonard Smithers in 1898, the year in which he died at the age of twenty-six. Infected, as he was, with tuberculosis, his imaginative powers were heightened and concentrated to an extraordinary extent.

Beardsley was an isolated phenomenon. He was essentially a decorator, yet he was in most ways a literary artist. He never looked at life, except through the distorting glasses of literature, music or art. None of this literary quality was transmitted to the artists he influenced – for they were mostly very different kinds of people.

One practical factor that obviously affected the way Beardsley drew his illustrations was the introduction of the photographic line block. Until the 1880s all line illustrations had to be engraved on wood. Artists either drew on the face of the wood block in pencil, or their tonal drawings were photographed on to the wood. The professional engraver then *interpreted* in his own linear manner the original work, hence the tonal quality of line illustrations in the nineteenth century. With the introduction of the process camera, such interpretation flew out of the window. It was all or nothing. Phil May had pioneered the new use of the photo-engraved zinc line block. Beardsley carried its use to perfection, both by economy of line and richness of texture.

In a world that is highly conscious of the achievements of the nineteenth- and early twentieth-century artists in the so-called Fine Arts, a number of greatly talented illustrators have been virtually ignored. Charles Keene, the *Punch* artist, has had a certain amount of grudging admiration. Phil May, who was also a *Punch* artist, never received a better accolade than that of Whistler, when he said 'Modern black-and-white art could be summed up in two words – Phil May.' Beardsley, belatedly, has had more than his share of recognition. And yet there was much talent working for publishers in the first years of photo-line reproduction.

Heath Robinson almost came into the first generation of artists to be relieved of the tyranny of the reproduction wood engraver. The zinc line block had come into general use by the 1890s, but artists were now working to a new limitation. This was the insistence of the process engravers that the artist drew in a jet black Indian ink on a snow-white board (a somewhat inhibiting experience).

The habit of drawing at least one-and-a-half times larger soon became established, perhaps because this reduction tended to sharpen up the drawing. It also helped to remove any qualities of spontaneity, which in the graphic arts of the 1890s did not rate very high. Phil May achieved his simplicity and freedom of line by drawing on a series of overlays of thin bank paper until he had eliminated all unnecessary lines. Most artists at this time began their illustrations with a careful pencil drawing, just as if they were drawing on the surface of the wood block. They then, stage by stage, carefully inked it in. William Heath Robinson and his two brothers followed this laborious procedure.

The change from wood engraving to the process line block and the introduction of the half-tone screen to reproduce tonal drawings completely altered the appearance of magazines and newspapers in the 1890s. Editorial demand for drawings increased, and with greater demand artists were able to get better prices for their work and many more artists turned to pen drawing for their livelihood. Young artists with a feeling for black-and-white work have probably never had such opportunities.

Magazines began to proliferate. Of the established magazines, *Good Words*, *The Illustrated London News*, *The Graphic* and *The Penny Illustrated Paper* still produced good illustrations. *Good Words* had been started in 1860 and was the first magazine to publish a drawing by Heath Robinson. *The Illustrated London News*, *The Graphic* and *The Penny Illustrated Paper* all concentrated on news events. Of the new publications, *Pick-me-up* was first published in 1888 as a rival to *Punch*. By the 1890s it had Raven-Hill as art editor and Phil May, Steinlen, A. S. Hartrick, Caran d'Ache and Sidney H. Sime producing drawings for its pages. *The Sketch*, which first appeared as an offshoot of *The Illustrated London News* in 1893 and which had S. H. Sime among its illustrators, was later to become one of the main outlets for Heath Robinson's comic drawings. There were soon literally dozens of new illustrated journals on the market. Of these both *The Studio* and *The Poster* dealt with the graphic arts and showed the work of many of the contemporary illustrators, including Beardsley and Sime. *The Idler* and *Eureka*, which first appeared in 1892 and 1897 respectively, both had Sime at one time or another as editor. Heath Robinson mentions more than once the influence of Beardsley and Sime on his work. Volumes have been written about Beardsley, but S. H. Sime is an artist who today is almost completely forgotton.

Sidney H. Sime was born in Manchester in 1867 and was trained at the Liverpool School of Art. His sense of the ridiculous, his attacks on the conventions and self-satisfactions of his fellow men were reflected in much of

Influences: Pen drawing of the ringside at the Pelican by Phil May. Heath Robinson used the same solid blacks for many of his illustrations to *The Talking Thrush*, published by J. M. Dent and Sons Ltd, 1899.

Influences: 'The Woman of Cha'. Pen drawing by S. H. Sime. *Victoria and Albert Museum.*

his work. There was, however, an innate insensitivity in many of Sime's drawings, inventive and skilful though they were.

Phil May was the black-and-white artist who had the greatest following in England when Heath Robinson started his career. He was *the* popular black-and-white artist in the England of the nineties, and was the antithesis of Aubrey Beardsley. His was the seeing eye. The characters he drew were all the result of his shrewd observation. Phil May's work was in part the result of the influence of the Impressionists; Beardsley's clearly showed the influence of the Pre-Raphaelites, and S. H. Sime's was a mixture of the influence of Beardsley and possibly of even the Symbolists, particularly Gustave Moreau.

In his autobiography Heath Robinson mentions more than once Beardsley's and Sime's influence on both his brothers' work and on his own.

Influences: 'The Dream'. Pen drawing by S. H. Sime, from *The Sketch*.

At one point, referring to an early stage in his career, he wrote: 'Wood engraving was no longer used for the reproduction of illustrations. The zinc block necessitated a style which Aubrey Beardsley made perfect . . . Aubrey Beardsley, Sime, Walter Crane, Anning Bell, my brother Charles and many others . . . arose from those conditions. The influence that all those had upon me is reflected in my drawings for Edgar Allan Poe's *Poems*.'[1]

What Heath Robinson says about these various influences can certainly be seen in his illustrations to *The Poems of Edgar Allan Poe*; what he does not say, perhaps was not even aware of, is how Beardsley's style provided him with a lasting technique. This can be seen most of all in the telling use of white space in many of Heath Robinson's illustrations. There are other less obvious factors such as the use of solid black for skies (Sime made use of this also) or the treatment of floral patterns on costume, the use of parallel wavy lines for tone or local colour, noticeable in both Beardsley's *Rape of the Lock* and Heath Robinson's *The Water Babies*. Beardsley's all-over treatment of vegetation, foliage and flowers as in *Under the Hill* and *The Pierrot of the Minute* is followed up by Heath Robinson in his very lovely black-and-white illustrations for *A Midsummer Night's Dream*. Yet none of this is plagiarism.

Heath Robinson was no Beardsley. For one thing he did not have to cram a long working life into six feverish years. Beardsley provided him with some of the tools of his trade. Heath Robinson was a very professional illustrator, who yet had much more than a spark of genius inside him, but he belonged to a very different world from that in which Beardsley lived and worked. The extreme sophistication of Beardsley and *The Yellow Book* was quite alien to the Robinson family. Though no doubt Will saw *The Yellow Book* and *The Savoy* he was much more likely to have been found reading the pages of *The Studio*, *The Poster*, *Black-and-White*, *Eureka* and *Pick-me-up*.

In addition to the inspiration of Beardsley, Sime and the work of his brothers, the Japanese prints of Hiroshige, Utamaro and Hokusai played an important part in Heath Robinson's development as an artist.

The work of the Japanese artists, whose coloured woodcuts reached Paris in considerable numbers in the latter half of the nineteenth century presented a new vision to European painters. The interest in nature shown by the Japanese was paralleled by the Impressionists, but the Japanese simplified and formalized their landscapes, in contrast to the Impressionists who were bent on capturing the momentary vision of light, of trees in motion, water sparkling, figures bending. The Japanese, on the other hand, produced a two-dimensional, formalized realism.

[1] *My Line of Life*

Influences: Illustration by Walter Crane. *Pen Drawings and Pen Draughtsmen*.

'The zinc block necessitated a style which Aubrey Beardsley made perfect'. Drawings by Beardsley of 'Venus between the Terminal Gods', for his unpublished romantic novel *The Story of Venus and Tannhäuser*. 1895.

AL AARAAF

'The influence (of Beardsley) is reflected in my drawings for Edgar Allen Poe's *Poems*'.
Drawing by W. Heath Robinson illustrating 'Al Aaraaf' from *The Poems of Edgar Allan Poe*. Published by G. Bell and Sons Ltd in 1900, reissued 1970.

Influences: Richard ('Dicky') Doyle's most famous drawing, the cover design for *Punch*
drawn in 1849. Heath Robinson's fairies floating through his designs for *A Midsummer
Night's Dream* may have been inspired by this or other of Dicky Doyle's drawings.

The most exciting elements in the woodcuts of Hokusai and Hiroshige were their lack of any familiar perspective, the high viewpoint, the asymmetry of their composition and the frequent diagonal stress in their designs. Another factor, particularly in Utamaro's work, was the white space that surrounds his figures. Beardsley seized on this use of space and made great and successful use of it.

There was one other influence that Heath Robinson acknowledged. All those solemn round-eyed children that he so loved to draw had their forebears in Kate Greenaway's drawings of earnest little boys and girls. As his own family increased, the Kate Greenaway influence grew fainter, and the plump, blue-eyed Robinson infants began to make their appearance in their father's illustrations.

There is one possible influence that he never mentioned. This was 'Dicky' Doyle, the artist who drew the design for the front cover of *Punch* and illustrated a number of Victorian fairy stories. The streams of fairies and goblins floating across the woodland scenes in Heath Robinson's illustrations to *A Midsummer Night's Dream* are very much like Dicky Doyle's little figures on the cover of *Punch*, yet these illustrations are among the most personal and most successful that Heath Robinson ever drew.

Heath Robinson's first book illustrations were for modest editions of *Hans Andersen* and *The Pilgrims Progress* and a 614-page *Don Quixote* for Bliss, Sands. These were followed by *The Giant Crab and Other Tales from Old India* by W. H. D. Rouse for David Nutt, a collection of stories for children based on Indian folklore. The naïve yet humorous manner in which they were written made an instant appeal to Heath Robinson. His drawings for this book, however, are rather immature. The publisher, David Nutt, was later to be tragically drowned, trying to save the life of another at Melun.

The next book he illustrated was *Danish Fairy Tales* for Dent and *The Talking Thrush* for David Nutt. This was a second and most readable collection of Indian folk tales once again retold by W. H. D. Rouse. The illustrations are much more interesting than those in *The Giant Crab*, and for the first time indicate the true nature of Heath Robinson's work.

In the same year Heath Robinson did about 250 drawings for a popular edition of *The Arabian Nights* which was published in part form by George Newnes in association with Constable. These parts were lavishly illustrated, not only by William Heath Robinson but also by several other artists including Helen Stratton and A. D. McCormick. Will's drawings for this massive undertaking were a mixture of his work in *The Talking Thrush* and the drawings he was to do in the *Poems* of Edgar Allan Poe. They were uneven in quality with much use of cross-hatching, yet his individuality was beginning to show through. He also drew a not very successful cover design

**THE AXE, THE DRUM,
THE BOWL, AND
THE DIAMOND**

ONCE upon a time there was a poor
young man who went out into the
world to seek his fortune. He went
aboard a ship sailing across the ocean;
and after they had sailed for a year and
a day, suddenly a great storm arose.
The rain descended, and the wind blew,
and it blew so hard and so wild, that
the ship went miles out of her course,
and the skipper could not tell where
they were. And then, in the middle of
the night, a great crash came, and the
ship was dashed upon a reef. The
waves beat and battered it, and turned
it topsy-turvy, and the end of it

The Axe, Drum, Bowl, and Diamond 15

was that every soul was drowned except the poor young
man.

The waves washed him ashore, more dead than alive,
and on the shore he lay till next morning, when the sun
warmed him and woke him up from his faint. He got up
and looked about him, and wandered over the place, which
he found was an island. It did not take him long to

walk round it; and then he saw that it was a small island,
and far as the eye could reach not another speck of land
was to be seen. There were plenty of trees growing in
the island, with fruit and flowers, bananas and cocoanuts,
and springs of water ; but on the trees were no birds, and
no animals ran about on the ground. So he lived on the
fruits and roots, and did the best he could.

One day, to his great surprise, he saw a black thing in
the sky ; and, still more surprising, the black thing had no
wings. Yet it was flying, and flew nearer and nearer,
until he saw that it was a large wild pig. How could a
pig fly through the air ? He rubbed his eyes and looked
again ; yes, a pig it was beyond all doubt ; and it flew
closer and closer until it came to the island. He hid
behind a bush, and saw the pig sink slowly to the ground

Double-spread from *The Talking Thrush*, published by J. M. Dent & Sons Ltd, 1899.

Influences: Japanese coloured woodcut by Hokusai illustrating the mood of spring and the drudgery of work. Hokusai's overhead viewpoint is one Heath Robinson used.

for the parts. At the same time he was sharing in the illustration with his two brothers, Tom and Charles, of a *Hans Andersen* for Dent. In this he played by no means a minor part. The brothers were more experienced, their work more fluent and Will was still trying to feel his way, yet the best drawings in the book are his.

The very early Heath Robinson illustrated books such as *The Queen's Story Book* (1898) show practically no evidence of the artist he was to become. The illustrations might have been drawn by anybody, some reflecting the impressionist pen technique of Vierge, others with much cross-hatching show the influence of Gustave Doré or even Whistler. Yet, within a year, Heath Robinson's drawings for *The Talking Thrush* foreshadow much of the illustration work he was going to do in later years and particularly his own books *Uncle Lubin* and *Bill the Minder*. For instance in *The Talking Thrush* the drawing of the partially submerged bather who has just been bitten under the water by a snake, but thinks it was the frog whom he can see, is the prototype of many of Heath Robinson's sad-eyed victims of circumstance. On this occasion the bather suffered no ill, but on the next day, when he was bitten by a frog and saw the snake, he promptly died of fright!

In the illustration of the perfidious judge and the equally disreputable crow, the artist uses the high-angle viewpoint, of which he made such good use later on. Throughout these drawings he is feeling his way and experimenting with heavy black shadows on some of his figures or using a solid black for a coat or a dress, with no light or shade. He also uses a tall narrow rectangle to frame some of his drawings, which he was to use years later in *The Water Babies*. This elongated framework must have been due to Japanese influence. Lastly who should turn up in *The Talking Thrush* but Uncle Lubin, about whom more will be heard later. He appears on the title-page and at the end of numerous chapters, with which he apparently has no connection.

'The Monkey and the Crows'.
Heath Robinson often used
this tall narrow rectangle.
Illustrations from *The Talking
Thrush*, published by J. M.
Dent & Sons Ltd, 1899.

'So the Judge had to pick his
father's bones out of the gutter'.
from 'The Swan and the Crow'
from *The Talking Thrush*.

'The wise parrot and the foolish parrot'. Illustration from *The Giant Crab*, published by David Nutt, 1897.

Illustrations from *The Talking Thrush*, published by J. M. Dent & Sons Ltd, 1899.

'Oh, it's only a frog!'. Illustration from 'The Frog and the Snake' from *The Talking Thrush*, published by J. M. Dent & Sons Ltd, 1899.

Uncle Lubin found his way
into the pages of *The Talking
Thrush*.

'The Judge winked an eye at the crow'. Illustration from 'The Swan and the Crow'
from *The Talking Thrush*, published by J. M. Dent & Sons Ltd, 1899.

'Day was already beginning to dawn'. Illustration from *Mediaeval Stories*, 1902.

'Went in to pacify her'. Illustration from *Mediaeval Stories*, 1902.

'But our Prior spoke out with a right manful voice'. *The Queen's Story Book*, 1898.

'It was what the Italians call a supreme moment'. Illustration from *The Queen's Story Book*, 1898.

'And proceed to Waltham'. Frontispiece to *The Queen's Story Book*, 1898.

One of the first of his illustrated books that Heath Robinson considered worth any attention was Edgar Allan Poe's *Poems*. The illustrations for this were in a very different vein from those in *The Talking Thrush*. The book was published in 1900 by George Bell and Sons in Bell's Endymion Series of Poetry, and by the Macmillan Company in New York. Three of the companion volumes in this series on Keats, Shelley and 'English Lyrics' had been illustrated by R. Anning Bell, whose work had marked Art Nouveau characteristics. In the same series, the Browning volume was illustrated by Byam Shaw and the Tennyson by a talented woman artist with the impressive name of Eleanor Fortescue-Brickdale. Heath Robinson remarked that he felt proud to be in such company though he does not make it clear whether this was for the Art Nouveau connotations of Anning Bell or the social status of Miss Fortescue-Brickdale. Whatever the reason, he produced a very interesting if uneven set of illustrations. The unevenness comes from the fact that he was still not quite sure where he was going.

The double-spread illustration to *The Raven* called 'The Night's Plutonian Shore' is a very rich design. The figure of a girl lies floating in the sea, with the pattern of her swirling draperies repeated in the cumulus clouds. The blackness of the sinister raven swooping low over the water is repeated in the black sky above. The only thing that detracts from this illustration is the rather feeble border down each side. There are many other just as beautiful designs; for instance in the frontispiece, 'Al Aaraaf', a standing figure of a girl with a great cloud of black hair sweeping up in arabesques is almost Rossetti-like, both in the treatment of her hair and the carpet of flowers on which she stands. The comparison of Beardsley's design from his *Venus and Tannhauser*, shows not only the influence he may have had on Heath Robinson but also the influence of Rossetti, Burne-Jones and other Pre-Raphaelite painters on both of them. Another drawing illustrating Poe's poem 'Lenore' shows Lenore cradled in the arms of her lover and framed in an archway, through which willows and poplars are reflected in a still lake. These trees are very skilfully formalized in a manner that Heath Robinson was to make particularly his own. One or two of the later designs in the book are less successful but the book as a whole is a most interesting production. It has stood the test of time for it was re-issued in 1970.

To trace in detail each book that William Heath Robinson illustrated in his early years would be of small service to him and less to the reader. He dismissed much of his early work as immature but even among this early work there was a promise of what was to come.

'The Night's Plutonian Shore'. Illustration from 'The Raven' from *The Poems of Edgar Allan Poe*, published by G. Bell & Sons in 1900.

'From the Thunder and the Storm'. Illustration to 'Alone' from *The Poems of Edgar Allen Poe*, published by G. Bell & Sons in 1900.

'Lenore'. Illustration from *The Poems of Edgar Allan Poe*.

In 1902, *The Adventures of Uncle Lubin* was published by Grant Richards. It was both illustrated (with well over a hundred line drawings) and written by Heath Robinson. This is a simple tale for children about Uncle Lubin, a curious little figure, wearing a tall, broad-brimmed conical hat and a long overcoat. Uncle Lubin's adventures are mainly concerned with his search for his nephew Peter, a stout baby, who had had the misfortune to have been carried off by a Bag-bird (Heath Robinson's name for a pelican).

To aid his pursuit, Uncle Lubin constructs an airship, on the most logical Heath Robinson principles, with the use of a lot of knotted string. This craft becomes punctured in a collision with one of the sharp points of the crescent moon, so Uncle Lubin parachutes to earth, successfully using his high-crowned hat for this purpose. He then builds a small sailing boat which he names *Kraken* and sets off on his search again. This time the *Kraken* gets stuck in the polar pack ice. Undaunted, Uncle Lubin (on the same stick-and-string Heath Robinson principles) builds a submarine and searches the bottom of the ocean for his missing nephew. He does not find him but meets a shoal of little mer-children – forerunners of his illustrations to *The Water Babies* which Constable published some fifteen years later.

After various adventures, at length Uncle Lubin arrives at some tropical land and finds little Peter in the Bag-bird's nest at the top of a coconut palm. The tale ends with the words: '. . . and ran home with him as fast as he could'. As in any good fairy story, distance can be annihilated at the author's wish.

Uncle Lubin, according to his agent, A. E. Johnson, turned Heath Robinson's attention to the commercial possibilities of his own quirky humour. The book has one other point of interest and that is the typographic layout of many of the pages, which almost follow Lewis Carroll's mimetic typography in *Alice in Wonderland*, where the mouse said to Alice: 'Mine is a long and a sad tale!' and the tale moves sinuously down the page in ever diminishing type sizes. There is much besides this of *Alice in Wonderland* in Heath Robinson's work.

Grant Richards, next, with surprising perception asked W. Heath Robinson to illustrate *The Works of Rabelais*. Heath Robinson said about this: 'It is a testimony to the publisher's enterprise, at any rate, that he should commission the author of *Uncle Lubin* to illustrate *Rabelais*.' Grant Richards was indeed an enterprising publisher. He was G. K. Chesterton's first publisher, and he published George Bernard Shaw, Ronald Firbank and the Sitwells. He started The World Classics series, which, after his first bankruptcy, was taken over with some success by the Oxford University Press.

'Uncle Lubin was able to start on his voyage'. Illustration from *The Adventures of Uncle Lubin*. Published by Grant Richards. 1902.

'Towards midnight he got quite near the moon'. Illustration from *Uncle Lubin*. 1902.

'Holding his hat firmly . . . he jumped right off the moon'. Illustration from *Uncle Lubin*.

NCLE LUBIN once more set sail in search of little Peter, though not before saying good-bye to poor Vamma-dopper, and kissing him kindly.

For many months sailed he, till at last he came to the land of Chilblains, where he very quickly became frozen up. Mind you, he wasn't frightened in the least; but soon made up his mind bravely to continue the search on foot.

Text page from *Uncle Lubin.*

Grant Richards was bankrupt twice in his early career and finally sold up in the mid-1920s. His faults were that he lived too well and, from the point of view of successful publishing, that he loved books too much. But the worst sin of all, in the eyes of the publishing world, was that he was always under-capitalized!

What Heath Robinson made of this sybaritic publisher is not recorded. Of Grant Richards's reader, T. W. H. Crosland, he spoke most warmly. Crosland was the author of *The Unspeakable Scot*. He often took Heath Robinson across the road from the Grant Richards publishing office in Leicester Square to the Café de l'Europe. Heath Robinson wrote of Crosland: 'Bitter and scathing as his writing may have been, I always remember him as a genial friend and as one who gave me great encouragement . . .'

Heath Robinson also illustrated *The Child's Arabian Nights* for Grant Richards. This book was chromo-lithographed by Thos. N. Storer, a Nottingham printer. (The term chromo lithography means that the drawings were redrawn by the sometimes not-too-sensitive hands of the lithographer.) It is a garish, crudely-coloured book.

Uncle Lubin did more for Heath Robinson than to persuade Grant Richards to commission the illustrated edition of *Rabelais*. He also introduced him to the harsh but profitable world of commerce. It was because of Uncle Lubin that Charles Edward Potter, a business tycoon from Toronto, wrote to Heath Robinson, telling him how he had been reading *The Adventures of Uncle Lubin* and asking him if he would be willing to undertake some advertisement drawings on the same lines. This proved a successful and happy contact.

The Adventures of Uncle Lubin, according to the author, was not a best seller. The single edition it went through was repeated a quarter of a century later when Chatto & Windus republished it in 1925 and yet another edition has appeared in 1972. It seems to have some staying power. H. G. Wells, in one of his novels referred to *Uncle Lubin* as 'a rare good thing'.

Various books followed fast on the heels of *Uncle Lubin*. The two most striking, at this relatively early stage in his career, were the *Don Quixote* (his second attempt at illustrating this book), which Dent published in the same year as *Uncle Lubin*, and *The Works of Rabelais*.

It is a far jump from the swirling yet formal patterns and brooding melancholy of the illustrations for Edgar Allan Poe's *Poems* to the realistic drawing and scratchy pen and chalk work of the drawings for *Don Quixote*, or the very powerful illustrations to *Rabelais*.

The drawings for an earlier edition of *Don Quixote* that Heath Robinson had illustrated for Bliss, Sands (1897) are rather tentative. One or two of these drawings show something of the technique used by Daniel Vierge,

Influences: Drawing by Daniel Vierge. *Pen Drawings and Pen Draughtsmen.*

'Don Quixote went on his way exceedingly pensive'. Illustration from *Don Quixote*, 1897.

the great Spanish black-and-white artist to whom Tom Robinson owed so
much. In the Dent *Don Quixote* (1902) Will's technique is still not quite his
own, but there are one or two beautiful drawings, particularly one of the
old puppet player 'Master Peter', with hand on staff and a little monkey

'Master Peter and his Ape'. Illustration from *Don Quixote*. Published by Bliss, Sands. 1897.

in his arms. The other drawing shown here of the two aldermen 'Both braying at the same instant' foreshadows much of the mocking solemnity of his later work.

It is interesting to compare the two drawings of the puppet player in the

'Master Peter'. Illustration from *Don Quixote*, published by J. M. Dent & Sons Ltd. 1902.

Sands and the Dent editions. The Sands illustration is an effective study of
a standing figure in a sun-baked landscape (seen through Vierge's or his
brother Tom's eyes), the Dent drawing is a much more interesting portrait
of a real old man holding a sad little monkey.

'Heaven endued me with strength to push him down a precipice'. Illustration from
Don Quixote, published by J. M. Dent & Sons Ltd. 1902.

'Both began braying at the same instant'. Illustration from *Don Quixote*, published by
J. M. Dent & Sons Ltd. 1902.

'Surrounded by a motley band'. Illustration from *Don Quixote*, published by J. M. Dent & Sons Ltd. 1902.

Heath Robinson admitted that he was attracted to *Don Quixote*. He liked the picaresque form of the novel, in which form he had sent Uncle Lubin off on his adventures and later was to despatch the King of Troy 'along narrower roads' in *Bill the Minder*. The same inspiration lay behind his illustrations for *The Works of Rabelais*, which was first published by Grant Richards in 1904 in a very large format in two volumes. The illustrations were all reproduced by line block with the exception of the two frontispieces which were printed by gravure. The originals for these frontispiece drawings were drawn in fine black pen line with much intricate hatching and a wash of indigo over them. They were drawn to a very large size – actually 559 mm. high. The line-and-wash drawings were clearly difficult to reproduce and lost a lot of their quality in the later editions, which the Navarre Society published in a smaller format.

The freedom shown in the *Don Quixote* drawings was carried a stage further in Heath Robinson's illustrations to *Rabelais*. The artist in his autobiography said about these drawings: 'The illustrations of *Don Quixote*, for whom I had and still have a great love, demanded a different treatment, a treatment that came more and more natural to me. It found its greatest opportunities in *The Works of Rabelais* which I was now to illustrate. I like to think that this change in my work accompanied a change in my outlook on life.' One can almost feel him hesitating, as, always being fearful of being thought pretentious, he modified this with: 'At least it was more personal and derived its inspiration, not so much from the work of other artists, as from the subject I was illustrating.'

The *Rabelais* illustrations are broad, earthy, appropriate to the text, yet in no way obscene. The book may have seemed a curious choice for Heath Robinson, a retiring and fastidious man, yet his drawings are certainly not squeamish. He appreciated the look of a pretty girl's naked body, as his illustrations so often show.

There were lively portrayals of the various characters among the *Rabelais* drawings. That of the physician Rondibilis foreshadows so many of Heath Robinson's 'respectable gentlemen', double-chinned, fat-cheeked, heavy-paunched. Doré's illustrations to *Rabelais* appear to have had little influence on Heath Robinson. The numerous studies by Heath Robinson of individual heads that were used so often for tail-pieces are often fierce if brilliant caricatures following in the tradition of Rowlandson and Daumier. Yet they are just the kind of faces one sees today in the streets of great cities and in the inns and farmyards of country districts. Heath Robinson made nearly one hundred full page illustrations and over one hundred and twenty head- and tail-pieces for this edition of *Rabelais*. It was to be the last serious piece of illustration that he undertook in this first phase of his book-illustrating career.

'Ring, draw, reach, fill and mix'. Illustration from *The Works of Rabelais*, published by Grant Richards, 1904.

'An ugly old trot'. Illustration from *The Works of Rabelais*. 1904.

'They fell down before him like hay before a mower'. Illustration from *The Works of Rabelais*. 1904.

'Rondibilis'. Illustration from *The Works of Rabelais*. 1904.

'Having been driven back'. Illustration from *The Works of Rabelais*. 1904.

'His whole life was one continual dinner'. Illustration from *The Works of Rabelais*. 1904.

It is curious that Heath Robinson was asked to illustrate afresh books that he had so recently illustrated for other publishers. In addition to the two editions of *Don Quixote*, he drew the pictures for an *Arabian Nights* for Constable and another *Arabian Nights* for Grant Richards; and he illustrated no less than three different editions of *Hans Andersen*, the first for Bliss, Sands, the second in collaboration with his two brothers for Dent and a third (and incomparably the best) for Hodder & Stoughton.

In 1904 he illustrated a comic book for Fisher Unwin called *The Monarchs of Merry England*. The plates were crudely printed from 4-colour plates and had a large element of caricature in them. There was one amusing drawing illustrating 'Charles I dissolving his Parliament'. It was an overhead view of little black-garbed Puritans scurrying out of Westminster Hall, looking like a lot of black beetles. Puritans clearly appealed to Heath Robinson. In another drawing he had rank upon rank of them sitting stiffly upright in the waist of an improbable-looking *Mayflower*. They also appeared on the endpapers.

Sometime before 1905, Heath Robinson illustrated three little books for the publishers T. C. & E. C. Jack in the 'Told to the Children' series. These were *Stories from Chaucer*, *Stories from the Iliad* and *Stories from the Odyssey*. They were published in two different bindings, the cheaper with paper-covered boards, the more expensive with a cloth covering, gold blocked. They each had eight coloured plates. The *Iliad* and *Odyssey* drawings still showed signs of immaturity with Art Nouveau influences in the latter and something of Frank Brangwyn's work in the former. The *Chaucer* on the other hand had a very pretty set of plates, drawn somewhat in the manner of his brother Charles. An odd coincidence was that a *Robinson Crusoe* in the same series was effectively illustrated by an artist called W. B. Robinson; this was not a misprint for W. H. Robinson but was Will Bennett Robinson who was no relation to our Robinson brothers.

These little books were merely a prelude to the handsome 'gift books' that he illustrated in the next four years.

Chapter Three

The colour-plate books

Book publishers were not long in finding a use for the trichromatic process of graphic reproduction and in the early 1900s a number of books appeared with half-tone coloured plates in them. Many of these belonged to the 'gift book' class. This term was usually used in the same disparaging way as 'coffee table', which is now applied to books that are clearly meant for looking at and not reading. The same disparaging terms could just as well be applied to many Private Press books, whose value is enhanced if they remain uncut!

In fact, many of these 'gift books' were nice books, intended to be read. They were well made, well bound in fine cloth often with a coloured illustration plate-sunk on the front cover, surrounded by richly-blocked designs in gold and colours. Sometimes they had ornamental headbands and coloured or decorated endpapers. Inside, apart from the many black-and-white illustrations, the coloured plates would be tipped-on to cartridge paper or boards, often printed with wash lines round the pictures and covered with tissue.

Heath Robinson, who produced some of his best work for this kind of book, had a rather tart comment to make about them, though he first paid tribute to his main rivals in this field. 'In the first decade of the century, there began to appear that *de luxe* series of books to which Arthur Rackham and Edmund Dulac made such fine contributions. The appearance of these books was partly due to the three-colour process of reproduction. Unfortunately this method could only be used on a certain kind of paper that was impossible for the rest of the book. Consequently the colour pictures had to be stuck in, making the book a scrap book. This was not true bookmaking, but they were nevertheless handsome volumes.'[1]

This was an attitude put forward by the Private Presses and other followers of the Arts and Crafts Movement. The implication was that any 'hand-done' illustration, no matter how insignificant, was a better thing than the results of the process camera.

Most of these *de luxe* colour-plate books were covetable things to be looked at and to be read in the drawing-room and not to be roughly treated in the nursery. Of course, not all of them were intended for the young. Heath Robinson's *A Song of the English* or *A Midsummer Night's Dream* were intended for adults, but they could well have pleased all ages. There can be no question for whom *The Water Babies* or *Bill the Minder* were intended.

The first 'gift book' that William Heath Robinson illustrated was *Twelfth Night* for Hodder & Stoughton. This was published in 1908, the same year that Arthur Rackham illustrated *A Midsummer Night's Dream* and

[1] *My Line of Life*

Edmund Dulac illustrated *The Tempest*. Heath Robinson wrote of this experience: 'The work was a joy to me from beginning to end ... I tried to preserve the atmosphere of the play as I felt it. The philosophic clown appealed to me all through the work and I endeavoured to insinuate something of his philosophy into the drawings. The art of the book illustrator, as I understand it, did not consist solely in literally illustrating the incidents. His relationship to the work he was treating was much the same as that freer one adopted by a musical composer to his subject.'[1]

Heath Robinson's *Twelfth Night* was a handsome quarto volume with 24 colour-plates in it.[2] The originals for these were drawn about 560 mm. high on a Whatman board in rather sombre water colour and body colour. There is a marked individuality in the viewpoint of many of these illustrations, foreshadowing movie camera angles and often looking as if they had been shot from above. The 'philosophic clown' that Heath Robinson talks about appears in no less than nine of these plates. The most telling is the drawing of the clown, illustrating the words, 'The rain it raineth every day'. This illustration was used as a frontispiece by A. E. Johnson in his short study of Heath Robinson.[3]

Heath Robinson was feeling his way with these water colours. They are, on the whole, rather gloomy. It almost looks as if he had hit a bad patch of weather when he was drawing the clown singing in the rain, or the clown trudging along a muddy cart track, or the clown again singing 'What is Love?' in the murky shadows of a dark glade of chestnut trees. In some of the illustrations there are slight overtones of Dutch painting, particularly in the one of Sir Andrew and Marie in conversation, set as they are in the cool grey tones of a Vermeer-like interior.

There are very few black-and-white drawings in this book; they were only used for the title-page and for the half-titles to each act.

[1] *My Line of Life*.

[2] The later editions had 40 colour plates. There is a mystery about the contract for this book. It was made out by Constables but Hodder & Stoughton finally published it.

[3] A. E. Johnson, *The Book of Heath Robinson*, A. & C. Black, London, 1913

Half-title to Act I from *Twelfth Night*.

'Clown sings. For the rain it raineth every day'. Colour illustration from *Twelfth Night*. Published by Hodder & Stoughton. 1908.

'Through the endless summer evenings'. Illustration from *A Song of the English*, published by Hodder & Stoughton Ltd. 1909.

'The flash that wheeling inland wakes his sleeping wife to prayer'. Illustration from
A Song of the English.

In 1909, following the success of *Twelfth Night*, Heath Robinson was
asked by Hodder & Stoughton to illustrate *A Song of the English*, a collection
of Rudyard Kipling's verse, which had been selected from *The Seven Seas*.
To this end, he visited Kipling at Batemans, near Burwash in Sussex, and
spent a very happy day there. Heath Robinson liked the beautiful old
house and found Kipling a sympathetic and understanding author.
Kipling, who was the son of an artist and who could draw himself, liked
the drawings, and as a result of this Heath Robinson drew a further set of
illustrations for an edition of Kipling's *Collected Verse*, for Doubleday, Page
& Co. of New York. This was such a wide-ranging subject that he found it
an even tougher proposition to illustrate satisfactorily.

A Song of the English was an unlikely book for Heath Robinson to illustrate. It is a collection of Kipling's verse in praise of the seven seas, the
prairies and the far-flung Empire. Anyone less like an Empire builder than
Heath Robinson it would be hard to imagine.

'The coastwise lights of England'. Colour illustration from *A Song of the English*.

'The coastwise lights of England give you welcome back again'. Illustration from
A Song of the English.

'We greet the clippers wing and wing that race the southern wool'. Illustration from *A Song of the English*.

'But drops our dead on the sand'. Illustration from *A Song of the English*.

'The wrecks that dissolve above us'. Colour illustration from *A Song of the English*.

A Song of the English appeared in various formats, a large quarto with thirty coloured plates, an octavo with the same plates and another cheaper edition with no colour and eight of the plates reproduced as half-tones. The line drawings, in the same technique as he used for his *Don Quixote*, have a certain melancholy charm, but lack anything of the artist's real personal quality. Yet the drawings for this book grow on one.

In 1910 Heath Robinson reverted to black and white illustrations for *The Dead King*, a panegyric on the death of King Edward VII. This quite unreadable eulogy evoked from the artist some rather ornate decorative borders. For this book he returned to the style of drawing that he used in his illustrations to Poe's *Poems*.

'Or the wreck that struck last tide'. Illustration from *A Song of the English*.

Who in the realm to-day lays down dear life
for the sake of a land more dear?

And, unconcerned for his own estate, toils till
the last grudged sands have run?

Let him approach. It is proven here

Our King asks nothing of any man more
than our King himself has done!

Border design from *The Dead King*, published by Hodder & Stoughton Ltd. 1910.

In 1912, Constable published *Bill the Minder*, William Heath Robinson's story for children and the natural successor to *Uncle Lubin*. It was a handsome crown quarto volume, bound in fine green cloth-covered boards, lavishly blocked in gold on the front and spine, and with a four-colour illustration plate-sunk on the front, set within a gold border of rules and scrolls of foliage. Inside the book there are sixteen coloured plates and a hundred and twenty-six black-and-white illustrations.

In *Bill the Minder* Heath Robinson really found himself. The story is a simple tale or a series of tales about the wanderings of the King of Troy and a boot-cleaner called Bill, who became the Minder (today he would be called baby-sitter) to the bad-tempered family of a bad-tempered mushroom-gatherer named Crispin. Like most of Heath Robinson's characters, Bill was a solemn little person who took his minding very seriously, even to the extent of studying at the British Museum and in the Minding Room of the Patents Museum at South Kensington. Soon his fame as a Minder spread and he found himself minding a large flock of children. One day when they were out in the fields, being minded by Bill, they found an eccentric old man in a haystack. It was the King of Troy, who had been banished from his country. With Bill's assistance, the children set out on a journey, and through a series of adventures they restore this unworldly old gentleman to his throne. In the process they meet some very droll characters. These are the substance of some of Heath Robinson's wittiest drawings. For instance, the title-page to the story called 'The Musician' has an old man perched on a pile of rocks playing a concertina, with his music propped up in front of him by a gawky little fledgling; or the illustration to 'The Real Soldier' which has a bear-skinned veteran standing bravely up with his rifle under his arm, a great pipe in his mouth, three pots of jam strapped to the folded blanket on his back and a framed portrait of some female and a toasting fork nailed up on the side of his bear-skin.

Of all these illustrations, I think the coloured plate of 'The Respectable Gentleman' parading to church with his equally respectable wife on his arm and his dutiful daughter at a decent distance in the rear is the best. The expression on the face of this pompous ass is one of such ineffable self-satisfaction, the details of his clothes are so incongruously appropriate, with a great pearl tie-pin that sticks up out of his cravat like a flag-pole, a flowered waistcoat of immense flamboyance supporting a gold chain and seals and his betasselled umbrella daintily suspended from his podgy hand. This is a very funny picture, yet there are certain sombre undertones. One gets the feeling that the daughter may not be enjoying it very much. This drawing really has the essence of Heath Robinson's art in it. It is a very pretty design with, for instance, the roses in the foreground repeated on the dress of the Respectable Gentleman's respectable wife. In contrast it is

'Colour-plate books were covetable things'. The cover of *Bill the Minder*,
published by Constable 1912

deadly serious, as are the characters themselves, yet every detail reveals something of the comic ludicrousness of such self-satisfied respectability.

In one of a series of folders issued by Percy V. Bradshaw in 1918, under the title of *The Art of Illustration*, there is a stage-by-stage description of how Heath Robinson carried out such a coloured illustration. The six stages begin with a rough pen sketch. In stage two, the modified finished drawing is carefully drawn in in pencil on a semi-smooth Whatman paper. In stage three, the design is inked in, mainly in a fine outline with a Gillott's litho Crow Quill No 659 pen nib, which was not unlike a mapping pen. In stage four, a grey wash was put over the whole picture, this wash was made up of indigo, lamp-black and a little Chinese white to give it opacity. In stage five a darker grey wash was used for areas of shade; chiaroscuro effects were introduced by washing out the light areas with a sable brush, loaded with water. This resulted in a complete tonal drawing. In stage six, colour was introduced – in the same manner that a painter such as Rembrandt, working in oils, would have used coloured glazes.

Arthur Rackham used a comparable technique for his colour illustrations. A. S. Hartrick described this in *The Old Watercolour Society's Club's* 18th volume, 1940. Rackham would run a fairly strong tint of raw umber over his pen drawing, except for a few white areas where he planned to place some accents of pure colour. Hartrick then said: 'This warm tone he lifted with a wet brush as he went along working in the local colour as he wanted, while carefully watching the main gradations – warm to cold and vice versa.'[1]

The Art of Illustration was one of a series of folders that Bradshaw issued from his Press Art School. This was a far from contemptible correspondence school with various different courses in illustration, cartooning and so on. In this particular folder, Heath Robinson is quoted when discussing his comic inventions: 'I really have a secret satisfaction in being considered rather mad, when actually I am playing the part of an artist who strains with all his powers to suggest the absolute conviction, logic and solid reality of the things he portrays.' He continues: 'Technique must be naïve, and have all the appearance of absolute conscientiousness.' Referring to the preparation of his illustration in this folder, where it was stated that he used no models: 'Finally, I would add one remark with regard to the six stages [of carrying out an illustration]. I would not like it to be thought that I depreciate or belittle the value and use of models. I merely find that for my own purpose, it is better not to use them directly.' In this he is reiterating Gauguin's words when Gauguin said: 'It is well for young men to have a model but let them draw the curtain on it while they are painting.

[1] Derek Hudson, *Arthur Rackham*. London, Wm. Heinemann Ltd, 1960.

'The Musician'. Illustration from *Bill the Minder*.

Drawing on the fly leaf of a presentation copy of *Bill the Minder*. 1912.

'The Lost Grocer'. Illustration from *Bill the Minder*.

'The Real Soldier'. Illustration from *Bill the Minder*.

It is better to paint from memory, for then the work will be your own.'
Heath Robinson clearly had a very good visual memory and he was a good
draughtsman. This fact is often obscured by the intentional naïvety of the
drawing of many of his illustrations and particularly in his comic drawings.

Some of the originals of his coloured illustrations are not particularly
nice things in their own right. They were drawn and painted about twice
as large as the reproduction, for one particular purpose, and that was to be
reproduced by the relatively new trichromatic half-tone process.

Heath Robinson, brought up in the trade, knew all about this. He was
an utterly professional performer and left nothing to chance. This sometimes resulted in the original drawings looking rather dead, yet triumphant-
ly coming to life in the reproductions. The original drawing was of little
importance, what mattered was how it looked when it was reproduced.

The year following the publication of *Bill the Minder*, Heath Robinson
illustrated *Hans Andersen's Fairy Tales* for the third time, for Hodder &
Stoughton. He was, up to a point, a traditionalist, particularly as far as
Hans Andersen was concerned. He says about this: 'There are, however,
certain traditions in connection with the illustrations of fairy stories which
cannot be ignored. Gnomes and fairies, at least in all European countries,
have a family resemblance. An artist cannot invent an entirely new kind of
gnome. Perhaps it is this that has convinced many children, young and old
that fairies really exist.'[1]

The drawings for this edition of *Hans Andersen's Fairy Tales* are very
charming, particularly those in colour. Once again Heath Robinson shows
his liking for wet weather subjects. In his colour-plate for the story called
The Swineherd, the swineherd stands scolding the kneeling princess in
pouring rain. Kate Greenaway's influence is in evidence in some of these
coloured plates, particularly in those where there is an almost complete
absence of background. Interiors are indicated by a chair, a table and a
single picture or looking-glass hanging on the wall. The illustration for
The Red Shoes has much of Kate Greenaway about it. An old lady (the
shoemaker's mother) sits in a typical Kate Greenaway ladder-backed chair,
with the girl standing before her wearing the red shoes for the first time.

The Little Mermaid drawings, particularly those in colour, are an obvious
prelude to Heath Robinson's illustrations for *The Water Babies* which he
drew a couple of years later. Another colour-plate, a snow scene for the
story *Tommelise* with some very realistic drawings of mice, has something of
Rackham about it, but yet by the composition and the character of the
little girl begging for a piece of barleycorn, it is essentially Heath Robinson.
Among over 90 line drawings in this *Hans Andersen*, Heath Robinson makes

[1] *My Line of Life*

'The Respectable Gentleman'. Colour illustration from *Bill the Minder*,
published by Constable 1912

'The Ancient Mariner'. Illustration from *Bill the Minder*.

some very telling use of solid blacks for the skies, particularly in the icy cold scenes in *The Snow Queen* and for silhouettes in the illustrations for *The Marsh King's Daughter* and *The Emperor's New Clothes*. These are better than the coloured ones. Heath Robinson usually preferred his black-and-white work to his water-colour pictures.

Heath Robinson felt happier, so he wrote, with Hans Andersen's stories than with the macabre and terrifying tales of the brothers Grimm. Hans Andersen's fairy tales are gentler and more sentimental than the German stories, with which Heath Robinson had little sympathy. Arthur Rackham was the ideal illustrator for Grimm, and was at his happiest drawing grotesque witches and horrifying trolls and Nibelungs.

'The Wild Man'. Illustration from *Bill the Minder*.

'She ran as fast as she could'. Illustration from 'The Snow Queen' from *Hans Andersen's Fairy Tales*. Published by Hodder & Stoughton Ltd. 1913.

This delight in the horrific was quite absent from Heath Robinson's make-up. In his attitudes to fairyland he had much in common with Hans Christian Andersen, though if he had known the Dane personally, he would probably have found him as trying as Charles Dickens did, when Andersen visited Gadshill Place in 1856.

Heath Robinson expressed considerable pleasure in being given a third opportunity to illustrate Hans Andersen's *Fairy Tales*. His first attempt at illustrating this much loved book was in 1897. He later dismissed this juvenile effort as 'very crude'. The second time he collaborated with his brothers Tom and Charles in an attractive edition, that J. M. Dent published in 1899 (see pages 24–26). The third and last time was for the edition under discussion.

'The Marsh King's Daughter'. Illustration from *Fairy Tales from Hans Andersen*, published by J. M. Dent & Sons Ltd. 1899. Heath Robinson's second attempt at illustrating Hans Andersen's *Fairy Tales* in collaboration with his brothers.

'It was he who pulled her down'. Illustration from 'The Marsh King's Daughter', from *Hans Andersen's Fairy Tales*. Published by Hodder & Stoughton Ltd. 1913. Heath Robinson's third and last attempt at illustrating Hans Andersen's *Fairy Tales*.

'They carried the mirror from place to place'. Illustration from 'The Snow Queen'
from *Hans Andersen's Fairy Tales*. Published by Hodder & Stoughton Ltd. 1913.

'So Elise took off her clothes and stepped into the water'. Illustration from 'The Wild Swans' from *Hans Andersen's Fairy Tales*. Published by Hodder & Stoughton Ltd. 1913.

Influences: Drawing by Kate Greenaway from W. F. Mavor's *The English Spelling Book*.
1885.

'And made out of some old pieces of red cloth a pair of little red shoes'. Colour illustration from 'The Red Shoes' from *Hans Andersen's Fairy Tales*. Hodder & Stoughton Ltd. 1913.

Following the *Hans Andersen* illustrations, Heath Robinson returned to Constable for two of his most happy productions, *A Midsummer Night's Dream* and *The Water Babies*. In discussing his illustrations he said: 'Every new book to be illustrated brought with it its own problems. The Kipling books, *Hans Andersen* and *Twelfth Night* had to be considered from widely different points of view. The last was seen through a golden haze of Elizabethan romance, the Kipling subjects in the colder and whiter light of modern times. My edition of *A Midsummer Night's Dream* was published in 1914, soon after the outbreak of War . . . the old Greek stories of the wedding of Theseus and Hippolyta, of Pyramus and Thisbe and of life in ancient Athens as seen through English eyes bewitched me, all of these and their strangely harmonious combination with everything that was lovely, *and humorous too*, in our English countryside filled me with enchantment.'[1] This recurring sense of humour lifts these drawings out of the realms of pure sentimentality into which a lesser artist might so easily have slipped. Heath Robinson ends his remarks on the drawings for the *Dream* with: 'I was ambitious enough to try to express something of this in my drawings and make them a record of this, the most wonderful moonlight night in fantasy.'

It was a triumphant success and is indeed a very beautiful book. The commercial edition is handsomely bound in a grey cloth and blocked on the front in gold, lavender and indigo, with a pretty design of Titania, a classical statue playing a flute and two fauns frolicking against a solid background of trees. The illustrations, particularly the black-and-white are the best serious illustrations that William Heath Robinson ever drew. For *A Midsummer Night's Dream* he evolved a richly decorative technique for evoking a night in a woodland setting. One or two of these drawings are absolute masterpieces of penwork, such as the one of Demetrius calling out to Puck: 'Thou runaway, thou coward, art thou fled?' Puck is silhouetted against a dark sky. Demetrius stands under a thorn tree in a field of cow parsley. Or, again, the drawing to 'O heavy night, O long and tedious night', where Helena and her companions stand or lie under a great elm tree in a meadow of daisies and buttercups, with a pitch black sky behind them. In these illustrations Heath Robinson makes hardly any use of the modelling effects of light and shade. His figures are simple line drawings, with the slightest modelling to reveal the shape of a breast or the line of a thigh. In some of the illustrations, the artist has made use of the same high angle viewpoint that he used in *Bill the Minder*. There is one drawing of Bottom, Quince, Flute and the rest of the rustics wandering up the picture in a serpentine line, with no background at all. Apparently they are stand-

[1] *My Line of Life*. The italics are mine. J.L.

Detail to the same size as drawn from: 'Are you not he that frights the maidens of the villagery?' *A Midsummer Night's Dream*, published by Constable & Co. 1914.

ing on air, or at least on white paper, yet they are all quite firmly based. Heath Robinson uses a similar composition for the coloured picture of Titania and her retinue of little men with pointed ears, preceded by a baby boy blowing a trumpet. Here they are floating through the sky, but obviously on the same horizontal plane. The picture brings to light one curious anomaly of Heath Robinson's illustrations and that is that his old men apparently behave like little children and the little children like old men.

There are several very pretty coloured plates, including one of a tree-lined river bank, with Heath Robinson's inevitable foxgloves in the foreground, a Greek temple across the river and the reclining figures of Hermia and Helena 'Emptying our bosoms of their counsel sweet', but the black-and-white drawings are the illustrations that add such distinction to this edition of *A Midsummer Night's Dream*, and of which he was so justly proud.

'*Puck:* How now, spirit! Whither wander you?' Illustration from *A Midsummer Night's Dream*, published by Constable & Co. 1914.

'*Titania:* Playing on pipes of corn, and versing love to amorous Philida'. *Illustration* from *A Midsummer Night's Dream.*

'Hermia: Emptying our bosoms of their counsel sweet'. Colour illustration from
A Midsummer Night's Dream.

'*Titania:* Full often hath she gossip'd by my side'. Illustration from
A Midsummer Night's Dream.

'*Helena:* O weary night, O long and tedious night'. Illustration from *A Midsummer Night's Dream*.

'*Demetrius :* Thou runaway, thou coward, art thou fled ?' Illustration from
A Midsummer Night's Dream.

Half-title to Act II from *A Midsummer Night's Dream.*

Half-title to Act V from *A Midsummer Night's Dream*.

Constable published *The Water Babies* in 1915. This was a less elaborate production than *A Midsummer Night's Dream* but Heath Robinson drew a delightful set of illustrations for it. Charles Kingsley's 'muscular Christianity' and his moralising is not to the taste of this age, yet at the time when Heath Robinson's illustrated edition came out, most children took it as the bread beneath the jam.

Kingsley's description, at the beginning of the book of Tom and his sweep-master Grimes setting out at three o'clock on a midsummer's morning from the cobbled streets of the smoky north country town for the open countryside and Harthover Place seemed to be a promise of unimaginable adventures. The illustrations and often the slightness of them, such as Heath Robinson's drawing of this very scene, with the silhouetted figures of Grimes on his donkey and sleepy-eyed Tom tumbling along behind, were pictures into which a child could read as much or as little as his imagination allowed.

Kingsley's description of Tom's flight from Harthover Place after he had come down the wrong chimney into the little girl's bedroom and his run over the precipitous Harthover Fell and down into Vendale imprinted itself for life on one child's untutored mind, as well it should have done, for it is one of the most beautiful descriptions of the countryside in the English language. Here Heath Robinson wisely left the prose to speak for itself, except for one illustration of Tom being startled by a lizard. These drawings are much simpler than those for *A Midsummer Night's Dream*, with much use of silhouettes, solid blacks and open line. There are frequent thumbnail pictures set into the text, of subjects such as 'Tom playing leapfrog' or the gamekeeper at Harthover Place saying 'I was told to expect thee', and later in the book of 'Mrs Be-done-by as-you-did', ('a very tremendous lady she was'), or of animals like 'The Good Crow' or 'Two little birds they sat on a stone!' (These must represent the last of the gairfowl!)

There have been various other attempts at illustrating *The Water Babies*, most of them impossibly mawkish. In spite of the prettiness of the coloured plates in the Heath Robinson edition, there is a pétillant quality, a slight sparkling astringency such as one gets in a secondary fermentation of a fresh young wine, that lifts these drawings out of the category of just pretty coloured pictures. As for the line drawings, there is a profound humour in most of them. The drawing for '. . . and played leapfrog with the Town-Clerk', in which an immensely grave, very portly gentleman is leap-frogging high into the air over the back of a minion in striped socks, delights one by the sheer impossibility of a man so solemn and so fat being able to leapfrog over anything, let alone hoist himself high into the air as if he was bouncing off a trampoline. In contrast, the drawing of the pretty little girl with a garland of daisies in her dark hair standing barefoot alone in a field, is in no way a funny drawing, but it is a rather touching drawing. In *The Water Babies* Heath Robinson mixed these very different attitudes of humour and innocence with complete success.

It is interesting to compare these Heath Robinson illustrations with those of Linley Sambourne, who was the first illustrator of *The Water Babies*. Sambourne was for many years a political cartoonist on *Punch*. His illustrated edition of *The Water Babies* was published in 1885. Linley Sambourne had a curious wooden technique which was not made any freer by the trade wood engravers who reproduced his work. No doubt William Heath Robinson knew the Sambourne edition of *The Water Babies*, but it had little influence on his drawings, with the one possible exception of the Sambourne illustration of Grimes and Tom setting out for Harthover Place. Here Sambourne has the figures in near-silhouette, but with the lifting gear of the pitheads in the background. Heath Robinson's development of the Beardsley technique and the use of white space, brought air into these illustrations. The views of wide beaches and far-out ebb tides achieved by the most economical means seem to promise limitless horizons. In contrast, Linley Sambourne's drawings are tightly knitted and curiously claustrophobic.

The restrictions of war soon brought to an end the publication of the *de luxe* colour-plate books. Heath Robinson was now firmly established as a humorous artist and anyone who could make people laugh at the time of the battles of the Somme, Ypres and Passchendael was worth his weight in whatever precious metal you care to name. Will Heath Robinson missed what he called his serious work. This was not a case of the clown always wanting to play Hamlet, but rather a Hamlet who happened to have a golden vein of humour in his make-up.

Illustration by Linley Sambourne for *The Water Babies*. 1885.

'I was told to expect thee'. Illustration from *The Water Babies*, published by Constable & Co. 1915.

'And bade them begin in a lofty and tremendous voice'. Illustration from *The Water Babies*.

'Grimes rode the donkey in front and Tom and the brushes walked behind'. Illustration from *The Water Babies*.

Influences: Beardsley's use of white space.
'The billet-doux'. Illustration by Aubrey Beardsley from *The Rape of the Lock*. 1896.

'Up jumped the little white lady in bed'. Illustration from *The Water Babies*, published by Constable & Co. 1915.

'Then he saw lizards'. Illustration from *The Water Babies*.

'And every lass a queen'. Illustration from *The Water Babies*.

'The first thing Tom saw was the black cedars'. Illustration from *The Water Babies*.

'And played leapfrog with the Town Clerk'. Illustration from *The Water Babies*.

One of the last books with Heath Robinson illustrations that Constable published was *Peacock Pie*, a book of rhymes by Walter de la Mare. This is a modestly produced book in comparison with *The Water Babies* or *A Midsummer Night's Dream*. It has only one coloured plate but the black-and-white illustrations are full of charm and in some ways foreshadow E. H. Shepard's drawings for A. A. Milne's books. Most of the illustrations are

Illustration to 'Bewitched' from *Peacock Pie*, published by Constable & Co. 1916.

simple line drawings, often of just a single figure, but there are one or two elaborate ones that recall the *Dream* pictures. There is one to the poem 'Bewitched' of a boy following a girl, 'the lady of witchcraft', under beech boughs and once again through foxgloves, that is almost Pre-Raphaelite in the decorative use of foliage and flowers. For 'Nobody Knows' Heath

Illustration to 'Dream Song' from *Peacock Pie*.

Robinson has drawn a breezy scene of windblown trees and a small baby hurtling across the sky. This drawing and some of the others suffer from over-reduction in size.

It is curious to compare the Heath Robinson illustrations for *Peacock Pie* with those of Claud Lovat Fraser for the same book. Lovat Fraser's were actually drawn in 1912 – the rhymes were first printed in 1913 and it was not until 1924 that they were brought together and published by Constable. Lovat's gay little 'embellishments' as he called them were very pretty, but served only as decoration. Heath Robinson's serious little drawings really seemed to illustrate the poet's words.

The day of the colour-plate book was almost over. Perrault's *Old Time Stories* which his agent and friend A. E. Johnson translated from the French was published in 1921. It was one of the last of the gift books that Heath Robinson illustrated. There are some fine line drawings, particularly for *Cinderella*: 'The haughtiest, proudest woman that had ever been seen' and 'They tried it first on the Princess'. An interesting design, this, with the figures, as it were, stepping out of their linear frame; and 'The journey

Illustration to 'Nobody Knows' from *Peacock Pie*.

lasted seven years' from *The Friendly Frog* where once again he uses an over-head viewpoint and a procession straggling down the page. The book as a whole, however, has a certain slickness about the drawings and some rather Disney-like coloured pictures. The fresh charm of his *The Water Babies* or his *Hans Andersen* is missing. I get the feeling that this was just another commercial job for his agent, rather than the great labour of love his *A Midsummer Night's Dream* must have been.

'The journey lasted seven years'. Illustration from Perrault's *Old Time Stories*, published by Constable & Co. 1921.

'The haughtiest, proudest woman that had ever been seen'. Illustration from Perrault's *Old Time Stories*.

'Brandishing the cutlass aloft'. Illustration from Perrault's *Old Time Stories*.

Yet in the same year he wrote *Peter Quip in Search of a Friend* and drew a very gay set of illustrations for it. He reverted to the technique of the illustrations for *The Child's Arabian Nights*. The *Peter Quip* drawings were also chromo-lithographed but the result is very different from *The Arabian Nights*. These are vivid, bright pictures that any child would love. The simple flat colours are most effective. The ingredients of the illustrations are familiar, including the 'Bag-bird', the airship and a scene near the North Pole, all from *Uncle Lubin*, and a train crossing a ravine over a flimsy wooden bridge which was one of Heath Robinson's favourite subjects.

In 1923 Heath Robinson illustrated *Topsy-Turvy Tales* for John Lane at The Bodley Head. This was the last but one of his gift books, though its production was less lavish than *Old Time Stories* or the earlier books. It is in the tradition of his illustrations for *The Water Babies* with amusing and decorative pen drawings and some very pretty coloured plates, some of them almost Rackham-like in their muted tints of brown.

In a letter to H. A. Kennedy 28 June 1929, Arthur Rackham wrote: 'I need not say what a difference the war has made. The market is now divided up among stacks of cheaply produced and relatively inexpensive books . . . the difficulty of bringing out a rather better book is so great as to be all but prohibitive. . . . As a matter of fact the better class books do not sell half the number that they did before the war, and there is not as much profit to be made out of each book as there was, so neither publishers nor illustrators are having much of a time. The only men of my craft who are flourishing, are portrait painters and advertisement designers.'[1]

Rackham was stating a fact. The best work in the *genre* had been done before 1918. Heath Robinson had one more attempt in 1934 with his *Book of Goblins*, which was taken from Vernaleken's *In the Land of Marvels*. Though this book was quite expensively produced with gilded edges to the pages it could not compare with his earlier work. This is not to say his powers were waning, for ten years later, in the last year of his life, he illustrated a book of fairy stories by Dr Liliane M. C. Clopet called *Once Upon a Time*. This slim little book, produced under the stringent paper restriction of the 1939–45 war, was his last piece of book illustration. The drawings, admittedly only in black-and-white, are every bit as good as those he did twenty-five or thirty years earlier. Witches on broomsticks, flying horses and juvenile bell-ringers jostle with plump old men on penny-farthing bicycles, dancing pigs and a ladybird called Pugh. If ever a children's book deserved republication, this is it. It was a fitting subject on which to end his remarkable career as a book illustrator.

The economics of being an illustrator are nowhere better revealed than in copies of old contracts between Heath Robinson, his agent A. E.

[1] *Arthur Rackham.*

Johnson and the various publishers and commercial concerns that used the artist's work. The earliest existing one that I have been able to find is dated 20 September 1898 between W. Heath Robinson and Constable. This is for illustrating an edition of *The Arabian Nights*, which was to be serialised. The artist agreed to provide not less than 250 drawings, with a proportion of three full-page pictures to every 30 drawings. For this the publisher undertook to pay the artist the sum of fifteen shillings for the copyright and original of each picture, providing that the artist supplied not less than 30 drawings per month and that the drawings met with the publisher's approval. £187. 10. 0 for the lot was the fee!

In 1910, Heath Robinson was still handling the contract for his own book, *The King of Troy*. The publisher was again Constable. This time he undertook to write 16 stories, produce about 16 colour pictures and about 140 black-and-white drawings, cover design, title-page etc., all for an outright payment of £300. But on this occasion he got all the originals back so that he could sell them privately. By the time he had finished the book he had changed the title to *Bill the Minder*.

In March 1912 A. E. Johnson was handling the next contract with Constable; this was for an illustrated edition of *Hans Andersen's Fairy Tales*. For this the artist agreed to do 16 pictures in colour and about 150 in black-and-white for £300, the drawings to be delivered by the end of the year and the originals returned to the artist.

In the following April, again through A. E. Johnson, came the contract for *A Midsummer Night's Dream*. The drawings for this were to be delivered to the publishers by 31 December 1913; 12 colour pictures, 40 full-page line drawings (he actually drew 32) and 20 vignettes, cover design, title-page etc. for the same figure of £300. On the same day (16 April 1913) Johnson sent him another contract. This was for illustrating *The Water Babies*, where the artist was only called upon to draw 8 colour pictures and 50 line drawings of various sizes and shapes and a certain number of head and tail pieces. The outright fee was £200 and he had to complete the work by 30 June 1914. The publication date of *A Midsummer Night's Dream* was 1914 and *The Water Babies* 1915.

Considering the difference in the value of money today, these were quite good fees, but as Rackham had said, the day of the *de luxe* illustrated book was coming to an end.

In 1916, Constable wrote to A. E. Johnson confirming that they would pay £100 for illustrations for Walter de la Mare's *Peacock Pie*. Belts were being tightened. Apart from Perrault's *Old Time Stories* for which Johnson had negotiated terms at the same time as for *Peacock Pie* and *Topsy-Turvy Tales*, Heath Robinson's future financial well-being depended on Johnson tapping more lucrative sources.

Chapter Four

Improbable inventions and absurd situations

Humour to the humorist is a very solemn matter. To write about humour in anything but a serious vein would devalue its coinage. Heath Robinson himself confirms this in *My Line of Life* when, discussing the success of his drawings of inventions, he says that this was 'not only due to the fantastic machines and devices and to the absurd situations, but to the style in which they were drawn. This was designed to imply that the artist had complete belief in what he was drawing.' He qualifies this statement with: 'He was seeing no joke in the matter, in fact he was part of the joke.' To this end he used what he called 'a rather severe style', with no detail left out. He wrote: 'There could be no doubt, mystery or mere suggestion about something in which you implicitly believed, *and of this belief it was necessary to persuade the spectator.*' This is the key to the matter. Heath Robinson concludes: 'At the slightest hint that the artist was amused, the delicate fabric of humour would fade away.'

Humour is an ephemeral thing depending on customs, time and place. Nothing dates more quickly, as a glance at old numbers of *Punch* or the *New Yorker* will show. Some of the Heath Robinson drawings date, such as one of a device for removing a chaperone or his numerous jokes about domestic situations with parlour-maids and butlers. The drawings done during the two world wars have a renewed interest. Jokes about Zeppelins and Pickelhaubers or the Sixth Column and aircraft spotters might not seem to have much relevance today, yet many of these war drawings as well as his more personal jokes have a remarkable staying power.

When Heath Robinson started on his humorous drawings, he had some difficulty in selling them and on one or two occasions had some paralyzing rebuffs. One publisher said: 'If this work is humorous, your serious work must be very serious indeed.' However, he eventually found an outlet through the pages of *The Tatler*, though according to his autobiography, *The Tatler's* editor Clement Shorter was not at all sure how funny the drawings were. Bruce Ingram, the editor of *The Sketch* was his first great supporter in this field and more than anyone else was responsible for setting Heath Robinson off on his career as a humorous draughtsman. Bruce Ingram could recognize the qualities not only of a great humorist but of draughtsmanship in an artist's work. Ingram was a man of some sensibility who had assembled a very fine collection of drawings ranging from the works of Avercamp and Van de Velde to those of Constable, Gainsborough and Rowlandson. He must also have had a keen sense of the ridiculous. *The Sketch*, originally edited by Heath Robinson's future father-in-law, was an offspring of *The Illustrated London News*. It first appeared on 1 February 1893, with the statement that it would handle the events of the day in a less severe manner than that of the parent journal. Phil May was a regular contributor, as among many other artists was S. H. Sime, whom

Heath Robinson so greatly admired. Slowly photographs replaced draw-
ings until by the end of the First World War there was only one page left
for a humorous cartoon. This page soon became the preserve of Heath
Robinson. Among his first drawings for *The Sketch* was a series on 'The
Gentle Art of Catching Things', such as 'Spearing for Clams' or 'Tickling
for Bandicoot'. This was followed by other series such as 'Great British
Industries', for example 'Kippering Herrings by the Side of the River
Yare' and 'Oxtailing Soup'. Another series was called 'Little Games for
Holidays' which included one very fantastic game called 'Bouncing the
Beecham', and then came 'Half-hours at Eton'. He made one abortive
attempt at doing a newspaper comic strip for *The Daily News*. His hero,
Mr Spodnoodle was a reincarnation of Uncle Lubin in modern dress. In
spite of that he only lasted a few months.

Heath Robinson's work was soon appearing not only in *The Sketch* but
in *The Bystander* and in *The Strand Magazine,* for which he also did a comic
series about crime. Heath Robinson's work appeared in *Nash's Magazine*
(for which paper he did one or two brilliant covers for the Christmas
numbers), *The Royal Magazine, Passing Show, London Opinion, The Humorist,
Pearson's Magazine, The Graphic, Printer's Pie, The Evening Standard* and *The
Illustrated Sporting and Dramatic News.*

The design, the draughtsmanship and the content of these humorous
drawings are worth some consideration. For instance, 'Plucky Attempt to
Rescue a Family Overtaken by the Tide': the drawing shows the unhappy
father standing on a tide-encircled rock at the bottom of a high cliff,
holding his fat wife in his arms with their two children sitting on her back.
The rescue apparatus consists of a motor cycle tied to the back of a motor
car which is strapped to the back of yet another motor car. This conglomera-
tion projects over the top of the cliff and is held in precarious position by
eleven stout helpers and a twelfth beneath, who is supporting it with his
umbrella. A back wheel of the motor cycle is being used for a pulley and
the line from this supports a little man who dangles near the marooned
family. He is holding two forked branches to act as tweezers and is in the
process of lifting the first child off its parent's back. It could work, except
that the three vehicles could never have remained balanced in this precarious manner, and anyhow, how did they get on top of one another?
The little man with the sticks could never have lifted the child from its
mother's back, let alone have landed it safely on the top of the cliff . . . and
so on. The more detailed the description of the drawing, the more improbable the whole thing becomes. Yet, looking at the drawing, because of
its precise and careful delineation of all the factors, including the chopped-
down telegraph pole from which the willing helpers have collected their
rescue lines, one is convinced that this is a viable but complicated method

of rescue. The precarious balance, the literal cliff-hanger, provides the tension and at least part of the humour.

Unlikely balancing feats seem to feature in Heath Robinson's comic drawings. 'The Thaw' is another of these. One does not ask oneself how long that human pinnacle had been balanced before the thaw revealed them to the passing policeman. Perhaps their uncertain equilibrium was maintained because they had been frozen solid. Another drawing (not shown here) is called 'Narrow Squeak of an Alpine Touring Party'. In this a car that had plunged vertically over a precipice is balanced on the horns of a chamois perched on a pinnacle of rock. The car is steadied by one of its back tyres which has conveniently stretched out like a rubber band and is looped round the branch of a miserable bush that had a precarious foothold on the edge of the precipice. Another cartoon of the Ark balancing on a pointed rock on which her stern has grounded is a masterpiece of mechanics. All the heavy animals and a few light ones have been crowded into the stern to provide an equilibrium. The onlooker's belief in the balancing act is never in doubt. Heath Robinson was to use the same balancing joke for various of his 'Flat Life' absurdities and particularly in the drawing of 'How the Tenant of the Top Flat can Enjoy the Amenities of a Back Garden'. Here on the most precariously cantilevered framework, a contented gent sits in his armchair smoking a pipe, while his wife does a tight-rope act bringing out his afternoon tea. The equally contented baby in its cradle is suspended from beneath the chair.

Following another nautical tack, Heath Robinson's drawing 'Successful Outcome of Intelligent Precaution Observed by Old Lady in the Sound of Mull' saves the same old lady from death by drowning by the simple expedient of self-support by the use of a magnet held up by her umbrella and a lump of iron tied to the top of her head. By the laws of physics this ought not to work, but Heath Robinson makes one feel it would. He used exactly the same theme for another drawing 'The New Magnetic Life Saving Device at work on the High Seas', where a boatman hoists his badly holed craft well above the waves, by means of a large magnet on a pole, to the evident satisfaction of the two old parties and the little boy who are his passengers.

Though the term 'Heath Robinson' is usually reserved for some complicated contraption or improbable piece of mechanism, more of his funny drawings were concerned with unlikely happenings, such as 'Stiltonizing Cheese in the Stock Yards of Cheddar' or 'Landing an Anchovy at The Welsh Harp Hendon' or 'Remarkable Case of Absence of Mind in a Dutch Restaurant'. In this drawing, in an almost deserted restaurant, an absent-minded customer sits perusing the pages of *The Sketch*; he mistakes the bald head of the drowsy diner who sits opposite to him, for an Edam cheese

'Plucky attempt to rescue a family overtaken by the tide'. From *Absurdities*, published by Hutchinson & Company. 1934.

and cuts himself a neat slice from the shiny pate. This macabre drawing is worthy of *The New Yorker* artist, Charles Addams.

An element of the macabre is in the coloured strip-cartoon 'The Knock on the Door' which Heath Robinson drew for *The Graphic*. This cartoon shows how the soft-heartedness of an elderly couple in admitting a starveling fledgling to their fireside ends in the ungrateful and no longer little bird devouring his benefactors. There is something of Caran d'Ache's humour in this strip. Caran d'Ache, whose real name was Emmanuel Poiré, drew not only cartoons such as 'The Disappointed Nephew' which appeared in the Christmas number of 1888 of *Figaro Illustré*, but also drew the most effective silhouettes for *Chat Noir*. He might be called the father of the comic strip.

It is difficult to see any other obvious influences on Heath Robinson's comic work, apart from that of S. H. Sime. It was all very personal and was usually very gentle. 'The Professor's Love Story' is a case in point. The humour lies in the thought that such a gawky and unworldly peda-gogue could even contemplate such a human failing as love. A drawing captioned, 'A Warm-Hearted Old Soul Disguised as a Merman Seeking to Lure a Mermaid from her Native Element' is a more extravagant fantasy. The Old Soul, dressed in black jacket and striped trousers, sits on a beach with a salmon's tail tied to his feet and a winkle tied on to his top hat, fitfully twanging a little harp made up from two umbrellas strung together. The pretty little mermaid sits on a rock combing her hair and looking a little perplexed as well she may. On the top of the cliff is the Warm-Hearted Old Soul's two-seater motor car and the remains of his picnic lunch, which brings a note of reality to the scene.

'The Noble Effort by the Italian Colony in London to make a "Do" of the Italian Exhibition at Burlington House' was drawn in February 1930 for *Passing Show*. It was during the winter show of Italian Art at the Royal Academy. This drawing shows Heath Robinson's instinctive sense of perspective. Everybody from the top-hatted gentleman in the foreground to the musicians on the right of the picture and figures in the further room are firmly standing on the same plane – which is nothing but white paper.

'A Christmas Deed of Kindness', a colour gouache drawing for *Hutchinson's Magazine*, was obviously drawn with great enjoyment. It is a supreme example of Heath Robinson's humour. The utter improbability of the broken-backed bridge being held up by a little man balancing in the crotch of a long stick, which is held up by another little man standing up to his middle in icy water, does not in any way detract from one's belief in the kindness of the act. The thought of the countryman driving his old horse and cart, grossly overladen with Christmas fare, over that bridge even when it was in good order does not bear contemplation.

'A Christmas Deed of Kindness'
Hutchinson's Magazine

'Remarkable case of absence of mind in a Dutch restaurant'. *The Sketch*.

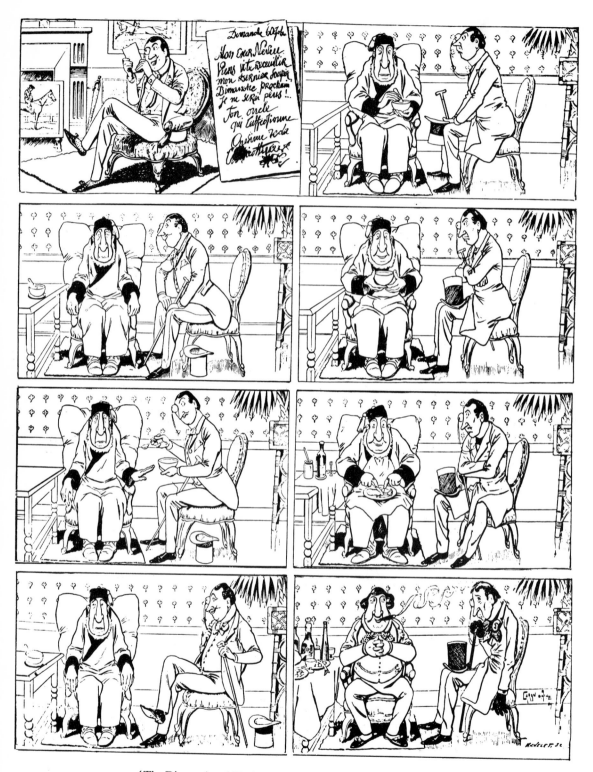

'The Disappointed Nephew' by Caran d'Ache. *Figaro Illustré*, 1888. The story strip method which Heath Robinson used in 'The Knock on the Door'.

'The Knock on the Door'. *The Graphic*. This drawing shows the influence of Caran d'Ache's story strip.

'The Fossil Hunters'. Drawing for the 'Piccadilly' competition.

'Low Tide' is a subtly tinted cartoon that might almost have been drawn by Hokusai. Two drunken line-fishermen lie asleep in their boat, left stranded amidst acres of drying sands. The boat is surrounded by empty whisky bottles, shamefully revealed by the receding tide. Three small children stand staring at the drunks with that disconcerting way they have. They foreshadow the urchins in Carl Giles's cartoons. The high skyline and limitless sands are reminiscent of some of the drawings in *The Water Babies* (see page 209).

The best of these comic drawings have a remarkable quality both of draughtsmanship and of observation. Like all great artists Heath Robinson enlarges our vision. That he had the vision of a child makes his improbable situations and absurd inventions all the more credible.

As for the Inventions, they range from 'A Simple Device for Removing the Wart from the Top of the Head' or 'A Machine for Testing Artificial Teeth in a Modern Tooth Works' to a method for 'Trapping the Clothes Moth in the Wilds of Idaho'. The latter invention consisted of a number of vertical poles from which were suspended upturned bath tubs below which hung some moth-eaten garments. At the foot of each pole was a bundle of hay concealing each individual operator, who could with the sharp flick of a knife cut the supporting string thus bringing the bath tub down on top of the old pair of trousers or whatever the garment was, and trapping the moths beneath it. Why the Wilds of Idaho should be plagued with clothes moths, or why such desperate expedients should be taken to dispose of them is something Heath Robinson's public never questioned.

Illustrations from *The Home-Made Car*. Published by Gerald Duckworth. 1921.

'Trapping the clothes-moth in the Wilds of Idaho'. From *Absurdities* published by
Hutchinson & Company. 1934.

'Noble effort by the Italian Colony in London to make a "Do" of the Italian Exhibition at Burlington House'. *Passing Show.* 1930.

'The Thaw'. *The Humorist*.

'Professor Branestawm tests his burglar-catching machine'. Illustration from
The Incredible Adventures of Professor Branestawm. Published by John Lane. 1933

The illustrations for *The Incredible Adventures of Professor Branestawm* were
drawn about thirty years after 'The Professor's Love Story'. The sentimental pedagogue has given place to an eccentric inventor, but complicated
and amusing as are the drawings, Heath Robinson was happier illustrating
his own ideas. How much collaboration there was in this book between
author and artist is not clear.

'The Professor's Love Story'. *The Sketch*.

Such personal and idiosyncratic humour was too good a thing for the advertising man to neglect. Heath Robinson's first commercial work followed on the publication of *Uncle Lubin*. This was for the Lamson Paragon Supply Company of Toronto in the early 1900s. It was not until after 1918 that he became deeply involved in advertising.

His customers included every kind of industry. One firm was Newton Chambers & Co Ltd of Thorncliff, near Sheffield. Heath Robinson visited their factory and watched with amazement the way use was made of the various by-products of coal. The conversion of a ton of coal into a bottle of mouth-wash or a tube of shaving-cream struck him as frankly miraculous. He wrote after visiting Newton Chambers, 'I have often thought of suggesting a scheme to them for reversing the process and re-converting the by-products back into coal again.'[1]

Heath Robinson's customers ranged from cement manufacturers to structural engineers and from swiss roll bakeries to tanners and curriers. He did at least half a dozen annual booklets for the curriers, Connolly Bros. of London. The word 'curriers' has a reassuring, old-fashioned sound about it and he obviously enjoyed himself working out ideas for every possible and impossible part of the processing of leather, such as the drawing 'Intelligent Precautions to Prevent Scratching of Hides by Barbed Wire, Thorns, Thistles etc.' with cows wrapped in eiderdowns and mattresses and the thistles covered in top hats; or in another drawing 'Nothing Takes the Place of Leather', he shows a kitchen table, a bath tub and a towel doing duty for a motor car hood. In one of the booklets, called *Connolly Land* Heath Robinson drew in colour a fold-out chart, showing just what went on in this leathery paradise. It is packed with detail, including the 'palatial offices' (a mixture of the Mosque at Woking and the old Euston Station), a 'Cow Sanitorium', the river Wandle with a boat under sail approaching at speed an impassable bridge, a bathing-pool with the 'Wandle Monster' and a justifiably alarmed bather, and a cricket match with a stout batsman being struck on the seat by a Connolly cricket ball. In addition to all this there are a railway train, lorries and aeroplanes all loaded with Connolly hides.

He used this fold-out technique in *The Gentle Art of Reproducing* for The Practical Etching Service of London. In this booklet he surpassed himself with some delightful drawings of the various stages of photo-mechanical etching (in itself a singularly unfunny occupation), starting with the reception of the original artwork from the customer who is being plied with whisky and cigars, through the various stages of the process and ending with the final fold-out entitled 'Prompt Delivery'. This drawing shows an aeroplane dropping parcels of etched plates on to the rooftops

[1] *My Line of Life*

'Coating the plate with a carefully mixed solution of fish glue, white of egg, etc.'
Illustration for *The Gentle Art of Reproducing* 1930. Practical Etching Service Ltd.

'Coke Grading by Heath Robinson'. Illustration from *This Coke Business*. Robert Cort and Sons Ltd. Reading.

'If there were no leather motor hoods'. Illustration from *Nothing takes the place of leather*. Connolly Bros. (Curriers) Ltd.

and into the eager hands of publishers, printers and advertisers. In the background of this brightly coloured drawing is the sober silhouette of St Paul's Cathedral.

A. E. Johnson tapped some most unlikely sources amongst these commercial customers, including the manufacturers of coke-grading machinery, wire-rope makers, walking dragline constructors and clothing manufacturers. For the latter Heath Robinson did an amusing set of architectural drawings of both interiors and exteriors of the emporium of Messrs Moss Bros. of Covent Garden, famous as hirers-out of wedding apparel. In *Then and Now* he let his fancy wander through the warehouses of the Port of Manchester. This booklet is illustrated both with Heath Robinson's drawings and with some archaic photographs of the same warehouses. In some cases the photographs could be almost mistaken for Heath Robinson drawings, so persuasive is his vision. It is a wonder that this gentle anarchist did not sow the seeds of dissolution through the various industries and commercial undertakings for whom he worked, or perhaps he did.

'Intelligent precautions to prevent scratching of hides by barbed wire, thistles, thorns etc.' Illustration from *Connolly Land*. Connolly Bros. (Curriers) Ltd.

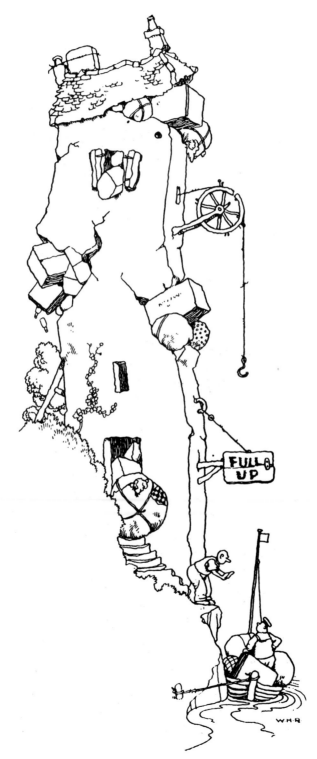

'Lack of accommodation in an old-fashioned warehouse'. Illustration from *Then and Now*. Port of Manchester Warehouses Ltd.

'Stages in the Production'. Illustration from *The Making of Asbestos Cement Roofings*.
Asbestos Cement Building Products Ltd.

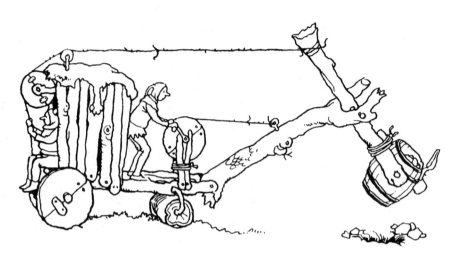

'The inventor of the mechanical shovel'. Illustration from *The Gentle Art of Excavating*. Ruston-Bucyrus Ltd.

One of his happiest assaults on the solemn edifices of the business world was his centenary booklet for The Great Western Railway. If any vindication was needed for private management as opposed to state ownership, Heath Robinson's Great Western Railway Centenary Book *Railway Ribaldry* provided it. That this great railway company should turn to Heath Robinson for its celebratory panegyric shows a splendid sense of proportion.

The paper-covered book contains some very funny drawings, including the frontispiece of 'Mr W. Heath Robinson's Own Private Railway Engine, Not Often Allowed on the G.W.R.', which was hardly surprising for it was a most gimcrack affair with wobbly wooden wheels, yet it still had an air of credibility about it. The other drawings in *Railway Ribaldry* reveal every kind of probable and improbable thing that could have happened on the Great Western Railway. 'The Building of the Saltash Bridge' and 'The Excavations for the Severn Tunnel', with in each case a sectional view of the sea bed and the earth's crust, are wonderful conceptions of bold and busy enterprise. On every one of the 96 pages in this centenary celebration booklet, there are solemn little men going about their tasks of building the first locomotive, testing the speed of engines, catching cows with a feather-bedded cow-catcher, teaching the meaning of signals to engine drivers (who are mounted on 'hobby-horse' engines), or 'Making a Simple Error of Judgement in a Goods Yard'. This last subject was a picture of a high loaded truck, with a man perched on top, about to pass under a very low bridge – and so on. The book sold for one shilling. Heath Robinson's public really got good value for their money.

'Mr W. Heath Robinson's Own Private Railway Engine, Not Often Allowed on the
G.W.R.' Illustration from *Railway Ribaldry*. 1935. Great Western Railway.

'The building of the Saltash Bridge'. Illustration from *Railway Ribaldry*. 1935. Great
Western Railway.

'Sectional view of the excavations for the Severn Tunnel, showing the hard and fossiliferous nature of the ground to be penetrated'. Illustration from *Railway Ribaldry*.

'Building the first locomotive'. Illustration from *Railway Ribaldry*. 1935. Great Western Railway.

In about 1933 A. E. Johnson submitted to the Bodley Head an idea for a book of Heath Robinson's comic drawings. This was to be entitled *Absolutely Absurd!* The mock-up for the first couple of dozen pages is still on the Bodley Head files. The drawings spanned over twenty years including two pre-1914 cartoons for *The Sketch*. One of these was called 'Stiltonizing cheese in the Stockyards of Cheshire' and the other 'The Ice-Hole Clam-spearer for use in the Frozen North.' There were also some amusing colour cartoons for ideal homes from *The Sketch*, including 'The Folding Garden' and one or two others that appeared in his book *Absurdities*. This mock-up was probably the first suggestion for this book. The second part of the projected book was to be sub-titled 'The Improvement of Industry' and was to show drawings advertising Hovis Bread, Mackintoshs' Toffee, Ransome's Lawnmowers, the activities of the Limmer and Trinidad Lake Asphalt and various other firms. It is a pity that a book of his commercial drawings was never produced.

Heath Robinson wrote about this side of his work in the mock-up. 'A Prefatory Note, in mock serious vein, introduces a section comprising a selection of the many drawings which the artist has executed, for advertising purposes, on behalf of different industrial and commercial firms, and which were among the more successful of the artist's efforts.'

They certainly were! The more serious the business undertaking, the funnier his drawings became.

In 1936, the year after the publication of *Railway Ribaldry* Heath Robinson collaborated with Kenneth R. G. Browne on a little book *How to live in a Flat*. This was followed by *How to be a Perfect Husband, How to Make a Garden Grow* and *How to be a Motorist*, all with the same author. These books were most successful and it was a happy partnership as author and artist planned the books together from the very beginning. Browne obviously knew something about artists for he was the son of the illustrator Gordon Browne, and grandson of the Dickens illustrator Phiz (Hablôt K. Browne). After K. R. G. Browne's death, Heath Robinson found another successful collaborator in Cecil Hunt and did three books with him. These came out at the beginning of the Second World War. The comic drawings he did in both world wars are worth a chapter to themselves.

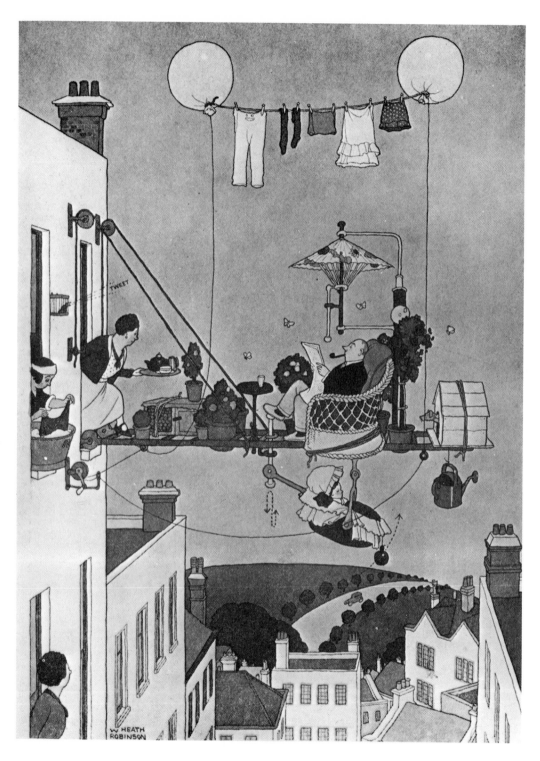

'Flat Life. How the tenant of the top flat can enjoy all the amenities of a back garden'.
Absurdities, published by Hutchinson & Company. 1934.

'An artistic way of hiding an unsightly view from a flat'. Illustration from *How to Live in a Flat*, published by Hutchinson & Company. 1936.

Chapter Five

Heath Robinson at war

Before the 1914–18 war ever began, Heath Robinson was showing, in a series of drawings entitled *Am Tag*, what might happen if the Germans invaded Britain. One of these drawings was of a pack of German spies lurking in Highgate Woods, of all places, heavily camouflaged as trees, animals and birds. They were carefully observing the innocent activities of a little Boy Scout. This drawing was reprinted in a German magazine and was apparently taken as an indication that the British people were in a highly apprehensive state.

With the outbreak of war in 1914, Will Heath Robinson was probably better equipped to deal with the German War Machine than the British Army was. By the most economical means, he succeeded in reducing the enemy to a bunch of pompous poltroons. His idea of just how the German infantry dressed, or what their equipment was like, was a bit outdated, based as it was on pictures of German troops during the Franco-Prussian war. It took him some time to modify this viewpoint, which he abandoned with some reluctance.

His war drawings were mainly for *The Sketch* and *The Bystander*. Their success was even greater with the British Expeditionary Force in the front line than it was with the people at home and soon he had a large and appreciative correspondence from members of all ranks in the Army, Navy and Flying Corps, who bombarded him with suggestions for his drawings. Sometimes inspired by his correspondents but more often under his own inspiration, his fantasy reached new heights with such weapons of war as his combined submarine and zeppelin, the 'Subzeppmarinellin' – a really fearsome contraption that he showed attacking an elderly female green-grocer in a rowing-boat filled with cabbages and fruit. Bombs and shells rain down on the inoffensive old soul, while from the very be-barnacled submarine torpedoes are launched upwards towards the bottom of her frail craft. It is once again a variant of the old joke of using a trip-hammer to crack a nut. A rather different approach was used for Heath Robinson's 'Button magnet'. In this drawing the enemy with diabolical cleverness dangles the magnet over the British lines, so removing all the Tommies' trouser buttons, thus effectively incapacitating them and so forestalling the launching of a counter-offensive.

Heath Robinson's 'New Reconnoitering Mortar' was designed to show the ingenuity of the Hun. Perched on cannon balls, they would be fired high in the air and then as they drifted earthwards under their parachutes they would observe what went on behind the Allied lines. This was one of a series of drawings published in *The Sketch* in the autumn of 1914 under the all-embracing title of *Kultur*. Another example of the enemy's ingenuity, 'A Clever Ruse', showed how two German officers, disguised as a milk-maid and cowman respectively, carried a gun, disguised as the cow, past

'A Clever Ruse. How two German officers carried a gun past the British lines'. An illustration from *Some Frightful War Pictures*, published by Gerald Duckworth. 1915.

the British lines. To show that the British might also have an inventive streak, in his drawing 'The Trench Presser', Heath Robinson shows two aeroplanes dropping on to a trench full of Uhlans a long wooden platform through which are poking several hundred bayonetted rifles.

Many of these drawings appeared later in book form, in *Some Frightful War Pictures*, *Hunlikely* and *The Saintly Hun*, all published by Duckworth. From the last which was sub-titled 'A book of saintly virtues' comes the drawing of the German general rejecting the offer of what looks like a large steak-and-kidney pie. The artist titled this 'Conscientiousness: an iron-willed Prussian general putting away from himself thought of food'. In the background his hungry troops give him a round of applause.

Towards the end of 1915, Heath Robinson started on a series of drawings which he called 'Rejected by the Inventions Board'. One of the nicest of these is the 'Blow-bomb: a device for extinguishing the fuses of falling zeppelin bombs'. The motive power for this primitive blowing-out apparatus is provided by two Scottish pipers with their pipes harnessed to an enormous air bag. As the bombs with lighted fuses drop from passing zeppelins, the blow-bomb blows them out, thus naturally rendering them harmless.

There were even funnier inventions reserved for the American forces. Towards the end of the First World War, Heath Robinson was commissioned by an American syndicate to make drawings of the American armed forces in France. One drawing was of a new kind of mortar that shot a company of U.S. Army troops behind the enemy's lines. They were seated on chairs and attached to one another by a long length of line. Another contrivance, based on a suggestion from the front, was a gigantic American Suction Tank which was used to extract unwilling Uhlans from their dug-outs. Then there was a drawing entitled 'American troops taking a peak in the Vosges district'. This shows them literally taking it, a vast lump of rock with a few nervous pickelhaubered German troops encamped on the top. This difficult operation was achieved with the help of aeroplanes, tanks, a steam engine harnessed to a cart-horse and a man on a bicycle pushing from behind. The peak was taken to God knows where!

There seemed to be no end to his wayward ideas and he continued to receive suggestions for further drawings from the three services and particularly from Sapper colonels. This two-way traffic gave Heath Robinson both pleasure and encouragement and on one or two occasions provided him with ideas that he could actually use. But these occasions were rare for the humorous drawings usually sprang from something very much within himself.

'German Virtues. Uhlan General rejecting a tasty Pie'. An illustration from *The Saintly Hun*, published by Gerald Duckworth. 1917.

'The New Mortar for Bridging Chasms'. Illustration from *My Line of Life*, published by Blackie & Co.

'The American Suction Tank for drawing the enemy from his dug-out'. Illustration from *My Line of Life*.

'Noble concession to democracy. The Emperor laying the foundation stone for a new prison to be devoted exclusively to the lower orders'. An illustration from *The Saintly Hun*, published by Gerald Duckworth. 1917.

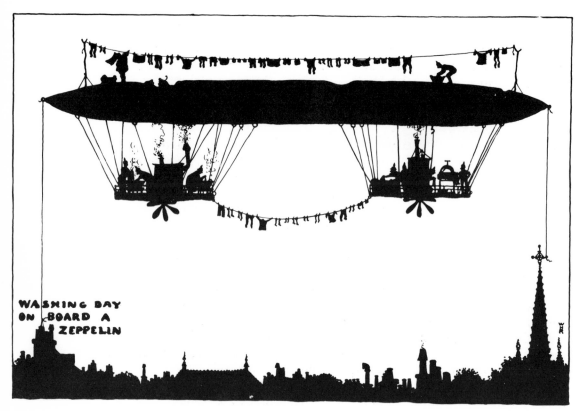

'Washing-day on board a zeppelin'. End-papers to *The Saintly Hun*, published by
Gerald Duckworth. 1917.

In 1939, Will Heath Robinson once again joined battle with the enemy.
The years dropped away and his cartoons regained the freshness of 1918.
In fact they did more than that, they were funnier and drawn with even
more spirit. The drawing 'Well camouflaged Home Guards meet enemy
paratroops half-way' is reminiscent in its viewpoint of his cartoon 'Catching
clothes-moths in the Wilds of Idaho'. The repeated use of the camouflage
theme in Heath Robinson's Second World War cartoons may have had
something to do with the fact that his eldest son Oliver was a Camouflage
officer in the British Army. This Camouflage theme in its deceptive guise
is used on one or two occasions, such as for 'Confusing the Enemy's sense of
distance or direction'. This was a drawing of German bombers trying to
bomb a representation of a landscape pushed up vertically through a
smoke screen; there is another, of our full-sized infantry lurking in trenches
with miniature models of churches, factories, vehicles and soldiers stuck

on top of their tin helmets. Quite clearly the enemy are taken in, so we believe it too.

'Armoured Pillbox Crackers for dealing with Pillboxes and other Obstacles' must have been drawn during the phoney Siegfried Line phase of the war. However devastating the pillbox crushers were, clearly no Germans are actually hurt. In the background, three of them are contentedly sitting in a truck marked 'Prisoners' which is being towed behind a tank.

The drawing entitled 'Some New Ideas for Arming our Merchantmen with Depth Charges and Other Anti-Submarine Devices', includes dropping old travelling trunks and tubs of stones on to a submarine that is sitting on the sea bed. The submarine's periscope is irreparably damaged by a scuttle of coal being dropped on to it; a telephone speaker is lowered down as a listening device and a shell is being aimed down a retractable barrel. Meanwhile life on both ships proceeds. A bottle of beer is being conveyed to the skipper of the merchantman and the crew of the submarine are eagerly awaiting their steaming *wurst* and dumplings. It is these little side activities that establish the credibility of so many of Heath Robinson's cartoons. He made frequent use of this 'double-decker' convention in his cartoons, showing both above and below ground (or sea) views. Other examples of this double-decker treatment are 'The Oasis Trap', the 'Anti-aircraft Activities in the Ruhr' and a drawing showing park statuary being retracted below ground during an air raid.

As well as dealing with the three armed services, Heath Robinson gave his full attention to what was called the 'Home Front'. For instance, his 'Spotting for Small Commercial Premises' is a nice conception with an 'aircraft spotter' mounted high on a rooftop in a rotating chair, with a very Heath Robinson windmill providing motive power for the rotation and a bomb ready to be blown sky high by compressed air from a number of speaking tubes connected to the various offices below.

In 1940 after Dunkirk, invasion was a constant threat. Heath Robinson solemnly warns the British of their peril with his drawing 'Daring attempt by a gang of spies to stop the ringing of Church Bells in Warning of Invasion'. By means of something like the 'tower' electricity maintenance men use for dealing with high street lamps, the spies are lowering a lighted candle into a belfry in the middle of a bell-ringing practice and so burning the ropes that support the bells. One unfortunate bellringer has been hauled up the tower and two others have been tumbled over on to their backs.

These Second World War drawings gave Heath Robinson great scope for his inventive genius. Yet however extravagant or devastating his devices were, his basic humanity always comes through and the enemy is treated with kindliness.

'Disguised anti-aircraft activities in the Ruhr'. *The Sketch*.

'Desert Warfare. The Oasis Trap'. *The Sketch*.

'Cleverly camouflaged anti-aircraft gun emplacement on the top of the Monument'.
The Sketch.

'Armoured pill-box crackers for dealing with pill-boxes and other obstacles'. *The Sketch*.

'Some new ideas for arming our merchantmen with depth charges and other anti-submarine devices'. *The Sketch*.

' Well camouflaged Home Guards meet enemy paratroops half way '. *The Sketch*.

Chapter Six

In the context of his time

Heath Robinson started work when the art of pen drawing meant something. Joseph Pennell's mammoth work *Pen Drawing and Pen Draughtsmen* was first published in 1889, with a second edition in 1904. Pennell, a rather cantankerous American, was Whistler's biographer and taught etching at the Slade School of Art. In 1889 he was bemoaning the scarcity of good pen draughtsmen in England, in comparison with America and the Continent. This was, so he thought, in large part due to England's belated acceptance of the process line block. In the 1890s *Punch* was still using wood engravings to reproduce Du Maurier's drawings. With the arrival of Phil May and Aubrey Beardsley on the publishing scene, things changed dramatically.

In this context, it is not surprising that Tom, the eldest Robinson brother, looked to the continent for inspiration. In his case he turned to Spain and the work of Daniel Vierge. The early years of this century were a golden age for illustrators. The renaissance of black-and-white drawing in England began in the 1890s and spilled over into the new century with renewed zest. Beardsley had died in 1898. He was the same age as Heath Robinson. His career had finished before Will had really got started. S. H. Sime was producing his weird conceptions, but these were soon to disappear from the pages of the magazines. The most accomplished black-and-white book illustrators in England in the 1900s were Hugh Thomson and Edmund J. Sullivan. Pen drawing, reproduced by the process camera and zinc line blocks, gave the public for the first time a virtual facsimile of an artist's drawing. It was a cheap process, so it served a very wide market.

Artists such as Beardsley, Vierge, E. A. Abbey, Sullivan and Thomson perfected very different but often elaborate techniques of what amounted to tonal painting with a pen. Heath Robinson assimilated all this both thoroughly and successfully. What he liked to call his 'serious work' stands or falls by his most skilfully worked pen drawings in, for instance, *A Midsummer Night's Dream*.

In trying to assess William Heath Robinson's importance as an artist and an illustrator, as opposed to a satirist and comic draughtsman, it may be as well to take a look at two of his most successful contemporaries and rivals, Arthur Rackham and Edmund Dulac. Heath Robinson's colour-plate books must invite comparison with the work of these artists though their styles were completely different. Rackham was essentially a pen draughtsman whose drawings often had a marked element of caricature, and revealed on occasions a certain insensitivity. Rackham came into his own with his coloured illustrations which were basically tinted pen drawings, but tinted in such a muted manner as to give these coloured drawings the appearance of being executed on old parchment. The coloured washes pulled the drawings together, tightened up their composition and turned

Comparisons: 'Whispering Trees'. Pen drawing by Arthur Rackham from *A Dish of Apples*, published by Hodder & Stoughton Ltd. 1921.

many of them into delightful things. Up to a point Heath Robinson followed a comparable technique, using indigo rather than sepia washes, but most of his colour work took on the appearance of rather sombre tonal painting. Both these artists liked drawing curious little men but despite the fact that he was a great comic draughtsman, Heath Robinson's little figures are less caricatured than Rackham's and more credible, as if he himself believed in them.

Edmund Dulac shared with Heath Robinson an interest in the art of the East. In Heath Robinson's case, it was the Japanese coloured woodcut, in Dulac's the gouache paintings of India and Persia. Dulac's coloured illustrations for such books as the *Arabian Nights* or even *Treasure Island* have a dream-like quality and are really very pretty things. In contrast, his pen drawings are of little interest. Of this trio, Heath Robinson was much the most complete black-and-white artist.

How to place such illustrators as these in the wider context of contemporary art is a different matter. To the academicians of their time they may have been 'small beer'. Most of these academicians are now completely forgotten. At a more serious level of art, these illustrators' lives overlapped those of Whistler, Sickert, Steer, Stanley Spencer, Nicholson and Pryde and of course many of the French Impressionists, Symbolists, Post-Impressionists and so on. Of course they do not stand up to this kind of comparison, but nor would Cruikshank and Gilray to Gainsborough and Constable. They were attempting very different things.

If one looks at the paintings of any of these illustrators, their lack of importance in the field of fine art is easy to see, even though Heath Robinson's landscapes and water colours give some indication of what he might have done in this medium if he had devoted his life to it. To judge the stature of these illustrators by such work is pointless. To them it was no more than a little occupational therapy. All these men were professional illustrators, and each had perfected his medium – the preparation of drawings to communicate some aspect of a text, for reproduction and printing and finally for binding up into books. By these printed pages they stand or fall. Their books are an adequate testimony, not the actual originals of the drawings for those books, and far less their excursions into painting. Illustration may be a relatively minor art, but Dulac, Rackham and Heath Robinson were certainly masters of it.

As well as all his comic drawing Heath Robinson drew some very gay covers for the winter numbers of *Nash's Magazine*. Heath Robinson did a considerable number of realistic wash drawings as illustrations to stories in that journal. These were often in two colours, the second usually being a rather sour orange. In the 1920s and early 1930s this type of wash drawing

'The Pedlar'. Gouache drawing for the cover of the Christmas Number
of *Nash's Magazine* 1929

Comparisons: 'Princess Badoura'. Colour illustration by Edmund Dulac from *Princess Badoura* published by Hodder & Stoughton Ltd. 1913.

Illustration to *Nash's Magazine*.

'Mother and Child'. Water colour drawing.

was used by a number of magazines. The illustrations ranged from Gilbert Wilkinson's brilliant if slightly bizarre drawings to P. G. Wodehouse stories in *The Strand*, to work of such artists as Stephen Spurrier and in a more realistic manner Harold Forster. In the United States the master of this *genre* was Norman Rockwell, who for many years drew the front covers of *The Saturday Evening Post*.

It was the largest and best paid field for illustrators and Heath Robinson was driven into it, no doubt by his agent. He made a surprisingly good showing, but it was hack work, and a sad waste of his great talents. Still, artists have to live!

'And some because they want to climb the Alps'. *The Water Babies*, published by Constable & Co. 1915.

So far I have mainly touched on the techniques of Heath Robinson's drawings, but this is just the framework. What is of greater interest is what he was trying to say, and what he was trying to say differentiates his work from that of his contemporaries. He was a very shrewd observer and commentator, yet he saw almost with a child's eye. This combination of shrewdness and innocence is what made him a great comic artist and it is the quality that breathes life into many of his illustrations. It is of course obvious in the *Rabelais* drawings, but it is even there in *Twelfth Night* in his water colour drawings of Sir Andrew Aguecheek, trembling in fear of a duel or just nervously saying: 'For many do call me a fool'. It is there in the *Dream*, with his witty line drawing of the rustics, Bottom, Flute, Snout, etc. It is there in *The Water Babies*, dotted through the text in little pen drawings of top-hatted gentlemen climbing the Alps and dignified house-keepers ordering the sweep about and boys laughing and girls crying.

And it is at its rumbustious best in *Bill the Minder*, with a mixed gallery of characters, such as 'The Respectable Gentleman' who was so respectable he had to have a good natured Boy Scout to think for him while he devoted all his energies to cultivating his respectability; or 'The Lost Grocer' who was lured away from his shop into a Rip Van Winkle situation, chasing a Druid-thief who had stolen a tin of snuff; or the poor old King of Troy, whose wanderings were constantly interrupted by his insatiable desire for coconut ice. Only in Kipling's *A Song of the English* does Heath Robinson seem to be somewhat at sea – literally on occasions – with drawings of wrecks and lighthouses; and somewhat lost in the wide open spaces of the Veldt or in the crowded cities of the East. This is not his world. The illustrations are, however, a considerable technical achievement.

Over recent years there has been a renewed interest in Heath Robinson's work among art students, even to the extent of some of them drawing in a similar naïve manner. The fact that many of these students have also been devoted admirers of J. R. R. Tolkien's *The Hobbit* and *The Lord of The Rings* may be a coincidence, but if ever an author and an illustrator should have been brought together, this was the time. Sadly it was too late, though Will Heath Robinson was alive when *The Hobbit* was published in 1937. Tolkien's hobbits were real Heath Robinson people, well-to-do dwarf-like creatures, pot-bellied, dressed in green and yellow and rather suburban in their tastes. The little people surrounding the pedlar that Heath Robinson drew in 1929 for the cover of the Christmas number of *Nash's Magazine* might well have been hobbits. He would have felt at home in Tolkien's magic world of hobbits, orcs and elves.

Throughout all Heath Robinson's work there is an amalgam of humour and solemnity. The serious illustrations nearly always have something pointed and witty about them, the comic drawings are always peopled by

'Low Tide'. *The Bystander.*

immensely serious little men going about their ludicrous tasks with an air of dedicated solemnity.

Heath Robinson was also a great satirical commentator, a fact that by his modesty, the intentional naïvety of his drawings and the apparent gentleness of his comments, he did his best to conceal. He not only ridiculed the tyranny of the machine but he also foresaw the lemming-like overcrowding of life in our cities and provided in his drawings all kinds of appalling city substitutes for an open air life. His absurd situations, his comic inventions and his ridicule of the machine, of the paraphernalia both of war and of modern society as a whole, have earned him a permanent place in the history of our time. His name has already passed into the English language. But beyond all that he was an illustrator of imagination, skill and wit.

If Heath Robinson had never done a comic drawing, his reputation as an *artist* might have been greater. To take but one example of his 'serious' work – his black-and-white illustrations for *A Midsummer Night's Dream*, these are amongst the most accomplished 'pen-paintings' that have ever been done. Yet if he had not combined his great talents as a decorative draughtsman with his very personal humour, we would have been deprived of such books as *Bill the Minder* and his illustrated editions of Hans Andersen's *Fairy Tales* and *The Water Babies*, which have delighted generations of children and their parents for the last sixty years. The fact that Heath Robinson could combine these disparate elements so well is what has made his 'serious' work unique.

Self-portrait of William Heath Robinson and his beloved cat, Saturday Morning.

Bibliography

1897 *Danish Fairy Tales and Legends of Hans Andersen*
332 pages, with 16 line illustrations by W. Heath
Robinson. 210 × 134 mm. Published by Bliss, Sands.
Bound in red cloth-covered boards blocked in gold.
'The work done for this was very crude' Heath
Robinson in *My Line of Life*.
1905 A further edition of this book was issued and
was used by the London County Council for presentation as a prize in some of their schools.

1897 *Don Quixote* by Miguel de Cervantes. 614 pages,
with 16 line illustrations by W. H. Robinson. 203 ×
134 mm. Published by Bliss, Sands. Bound in green
cloth-covered boards printed in black.
There was a further edition in 1902 published by
Sands and Co. This book, in common with other
Bliss Sands books was printed on a coarse paper. The
line drawings were printed on a poor quality art paper.
These drawings are very immature, with certain
echoes of Daniel Vierge, though Heath Robinson
makes use of solid black for the sky in several of them.

1897 *The Giant Crab and other Tales from Old India* by
W. H. D. Rouse. 134 pages, with 50 line illustrations
by W. Robinson. 203 × 150 mm. Published by David
Nutt. Bound in buff cloth-covered boards with an art
nouveau design printed in dark brown.
1900 A second edition.
These immature drawings show the artist groping
his way towards a more assured technique. Mr Nutt's
blurb for this series is perhaps worth quoting:
'Mr David Nutt's gift books for children, illustrated
by leading artists in black-and-white, sumptuously
printed on specially made paper, bound in attractive
and original covers, and sold at the lowest price con-
sistent with equitable remuneration to authors and
artists, and beauty and durability of get up.'
Among the other titles in this series was Oscar
Wilde's *The Happy Prince and other Tales*, illustrated by
Walter Crane and Jacombe Hood.

1897 *The Pilgrim's Progress* by John Bunyan. 320
pages, with 24 line illustrations by W. H. Robinson.
213 × 137 mm. Published by Sands & Co. Bound in
red cloth-covered boards blocked in gold.
1908 A second edition.

1898 *The Queen's Story Book* edited by G. L. Gomme.
446 pages, with 20 full-page line illustrations by W. H.
Robinson. 191 × 137 mm. Published by Archibald
Constable & Co., Westminster. Bound in blue cloth-
covered boards, blocked in gold.
1902 A second edition bound in pale green cloth-
covered boards blocked in gold and brown.

1899 *The Talking Thrush and Other Tales from India*
collected by W. Crooke and by W. H. D. Rouse. 216
pages, with 56 line illustrations by W. Robinson, red
and black title-page and numerous decorated initials.
197 × 140 mm. Published by J. M. Dent & Sons Ltd.
Bound in green cloth-covered boards and with an
illustration printed in red and black on the spine as
well as on the front board.
There is clear evidence in these drawings of the
nature of Heath Robinson's later work. William
Crooke was a Bengal Civil Servant.
1922 and 1938 Further editions.

1899 *Fairy Tales from Hans Christian Andersen* translated
by E. Lucas and illustrated by Tom, Charles and
William Robinson. 540 pages, with 112 illustrations
including a chromo-lithographed frontispiece and
title-page by Charles and 31 other illustrations by
Charles, 43 by Tom and 36 by Will. Bound in cloth-
covered boards with a design of *putti* printed in
several colours by Charles on the front board. Illustrated end papers. 194 × 143 mm. Published by J. M.
Dent & Sons Ltd.
Though less experienced than his two elder brothers,
the best of Will's drawings are the best in the book.

1899 *The Arabian Nights Entertainments*, 472 pages,
illustrated with several hundred illustrations by W.
Heath Robinson, Helen Stratton, A. D. McCormick,
A. L. Davis and A. E. Norbury. 273 × 210 mm. Bound
in green cloth-covered boards, with a design blocked
in gold and printed in black, orange and blue. Published by George Newnes by arrangement with
Archibald Constable in serial form, price 6d a part.
1908 A second edition was issued.
For the weekly parts, Heath Robinson drew a
3-colour design for the cover, with some perfectly
terrible lettering.
1911 A new edition. 436 pages illustrated with a
selection of drawings by W. H. Robinson, Helen
Stratton etc. with a coloured frontispiece and title-
page 216 × 140 mm. Bound in blue cloth-covered
boards printed in black. Published by Selfridge and
Co. Ltd.
This edition was badly printed on cheap paper.

1900 *The Poems of Edgar Allan Poe*. 226 pages and 103
line illustrations by W. Heath Robinson. 203 × 134
mm. Published by George Bell & Sons, London, and
the Macmillan Publishing Company in New York, in
the Endymion Series of Poets.
Title-page in red and black. Bound in green cloth,
blocked in black and gold from a design by Anning
Bell.
Further editions followed and it was last reprinted
in 1970.

1902 *Mediaeval Stories* by Professor Schück, translated from the Swedish by W. F. Harvey. 321 pages, with 10 full-page line illustrations and chapter heading illustrations by W. Heath Robinson. 194 × 137 mm. Published by Sands & Co. Bound in red cloth-covered boards, blocked in gold.

Another edition in the same year was bound in buff cloth-covered boards with a Walter Crane-like design by Heath Robinson printed in dark brown.

1902 *Dent's Andersen in German* edited by Walter Rippman. 220 pages, with 18 line illustrations by Tom, Charles and William Heath Robinson. 181 × 130 mm. Published by J. M. Dent & Sons Ltd. Bound in unbleached cloth-covered boards, blocked in brown.

These drawings, greatly reduced in size, were from Dent's 1899 edition of *Fairy Tales from Hans Christian Andersen*, which the Robinson brothers illustrated.

1902 *The Adventures of Uncle Lubin* written and illustrated by W. Heath Robinson. 120 pages. Coloured frontispiece, 55 full-page and 72 vignette line illustrations. Red and black title-page and red initials throughout. 203 × 152 mm. Published by Grant Richards. Bound in green cloth-covered boards blocked in four colours.

This, the first edition, is now a rare book.

1925 Re-issued by Chatto & Windus. 216 × 152 mm. Printed throughout in black and blue with decorated endpapers. Bound in yellow cloth-covered boards, blocked in dark red.

Not nearly such an attractive book as the original.

1972 New Edition by the Minerva Press.

1902 *The Adventures of Don Quixote of La Mancha* by Miguel de Cervantes. 532 pages, with decorated title-page in red and black and 44 illustrations in line or chalk by W. Heath Robinson. 194 × 146 mm. Published by J. M. Dent & Sons Ltd. Bound in green cloth with illustrations printed in black and yellow. Green endpapers with a design printed in brown.

Some of the drawings show the influence of T. H. Robinson and Daniel Vierge, but among them there are some very spirited drawings.

1953 A later edition 213 × 137 mm, was published by Dent. This volume contains 8 coloured plates which do no great credit to the artist. Some of the black-and-white drawings are from the original edition and some were specially drawn for this new edition. Not a very happy mixture.

1902 *The Surprising Travels and Adventures of Baron Munchausen* illustrated by W. Heath Robinson. 256 pages with 4 colour plates, 171 × 115 mm. Published by Grant Richards in The Children's Library. Bound in blue cloth-covered boards, with an art nouveau design blocked in gold. The illustrations are rather crude and are badly printed by the four-colour process.

1902 *Tales from Shakespeare* by Charles Lamb. 296 pages, 210 × 140 mm. Published by Sands & Co. Bound in red cloth-covered boards blocked in gold.

The drawings are very much in the John Gilbert vein. There is hardly a hint here of how his work was to develop.

The British Museum stamp is dated 28 January 1902, so it is possible the publication date was 1901.

It is a companion volume to *The Pilgrim's Progress*.

1903 *The Child's Arabian Nights* written and illustrated by W. Heath Robinson. 84 pages with 12 colour plates. Printed by chromo-lithography on heavy coated stock. Published by Grant Richards. Printed by Thos. N. Storer & Co. of Nottingham. Bound in paper-covered boards with a design of children's heads printed in several colours.

The quality of the drawings, which are printed in very garish colours, suffer from the clumsy hands of the chromo-lithographers, who redrew the artist's designs onto lithographic plates. This now rare book is quite unlike most of Heath Robinson's illustrated children's books. Some of the illustrations are reminiscent of modern Pop art.

1903 *Rama and the Monkeys*, adapted for children from *The Ramayana* by Geraldine Hodgson. 104 pages, illustrated with a coloured frontispiece, a decorated title-page and 6 black-and-white drawings by W. H. Robinson. 157 × 95 mm. Published by J. M. Dent & Sons Ltd. Bound in blue cloth-covered boards blocked in gold.

The drawings in this very small book are similar in style to W. H. Robinson's illustrations to Poe's *Poems*. The drawings are set within decorative borders.

N.D. *The Memoirs of Barry Lyndon* by W. M. Thackeray. 572 pages, illustrated by various artists including George Cruikshank and with 6 line drawings, two of them in colour by W. Heath Robinson. 203 × 130 mm. Bound in red cloth-covered boards, blocked in gold. Published by The Caxton Publishing Co. Ltd.

This was first published in 1887, presumably without all the illustrations, by G. Routledge, and re-issued by The Caxton Publishing Company in 1892 and 1893. At what stage the Heath Robinson illustrations were included is not clear.

1904 *The Works of Rabelais* in two volumes, illustrated by W. Heath Robinson. Vol. I (378 pages) has a gravure frontispiece and 54 full-page line illustrations and 65 vignettes.

Vol. II (350 pages), has a gravure frontispiece, 43 full-page line illustrations and 63 vignettes. 289 × 228 mm. Published by Grant Richards. Bound in heavy white cloth with a gold blocked design on front and spine.

The frontispieces are very fine pen drawings originally 559 mm. high and with a water colour wash of indigo. When printed by gravure, as they are here, they look like etchings.

1913 Re-issued by the Navarre Society. This is a scaled down version of the first edition. 228 × 146 mm. Vol. I, (476 pages), Vol. II, (464 pages). Bound in white cloth-covered boards blocked in gold. Title-page in red and black.

Frontispiece illustrations are printed by half-tone and compare unfavourably with the original edition.

Further editions were published by the Navarre Society in 1921 and 1948. These were trimmed to a slightly smaller size 213 × 134 mm. and bound in white and blue cloth covered-boards respectively.

1904 *The Monarchs of Merry England* (James I to Edward VII). Humorous rhymes of historical times by Roland Carse. 52 pages, with 10 colour plates and 45 line drawings in the text by W. Heath Robinson. 286 × 223 mm. Quarter bound with red cloth spine and brown paper-covered boards with colour plate on the front. Illustrated endpapers printed in grey. Published by Fisher Unwin and printed by the four-colour process by Alf Cooke of Leeds.

N.D. Later issued in four parts 279 × 216 mm., with saddle-stitched board covers printed in four colours and with colour plates re-lithographed by Alf Cooke.

1904 *The Merry Multifleet and the Mounting Multicorps* by Howard Angus Kennedy. Illustrated in line by W. Heath Robinson. 206 pages 177 × 121 mm. Published by J. M. Dent and Co. Bound in white cloth-covered boards, blocked in black and red.

1906(?) *Stories from Chaucer told to the Children* by Janet Harvey Kelman. 114 pages, with 8 colour-plates by W. Heath Robinson. 136 × 115 mm. Published by T. C. & E. C. Jack. Bound in brown paper-covered boards with a four-colour illustration plate-sunk on the front and the title blocked in dark brown. Printed by T. & A. Constable. There is the date of 1905 on the fly-leaf of the copy in my possession, though the British Museum catalogue gives 1906 as the date of publication.

N.D. *Stories from the Iliad told to the Children* with 8 colour-plates by W. Heath Robinson. 136 × 115 mm.

Published by T. C. & E. C. Jack. Bound in brown cloth-covered boards, blocked in gold with a four-colour illustration plate-sunk on the front.

N.D. *Stories from the Odyssey told to the Children* with 8 colour-plates by W. Heath Robinson. 136 × 115 mm. Published by T. C. & E. C. Jack. Bound in brown cloth-covered boards, blocked in gold and with a four-colour illustration plate-sunk on the front.

The 'Told to the Children Series' was edited by Louey Chisholm.

1908 *Twelfth Night* by William Shakespeare, illustrated by W. Heath Robinson. 144 pages with 24 tipped-in colour-plates and a half-title and title-page with vignette line drawings. 248 × 184 mm. Published by Hodder & Stoughton. Bound in blue cloth-covered boards blocked in gold and printed in green and brown.

N.D. A succeeding edition has 40 colour-plates tipped onto green boards and is bound in green cloth-covered boards blocked in gold on front and spine.

There was also a Limited Edition printed on hand-made paper and signed by the artist of 350 copies. 144 pages. 279 × 223 mm., with 40 colour-plates. Bound in white vellum and blocked in gold.

1909 *A Song of the English* by Rudyard Kipling. Illustrated by W. Heath Robinson. 128 pages, with 30 colour-plates tipped on to cream coloured boards with printed borders, and 60 line illustrations. 279 × 220 mm. Published by Hodder & Stoughton, London, Bound in blue cloth-covered boards, blocked in gold.

There was also a Limited Edition of 500 copies, signed by the artist, printed on hand-made paper and bound in vellum, with a design blocked in red, green and gold on the front board.

There was a smaller format edition (242 × 184 mm.) with 16 colour-plates bound in dark blue cloth-covered boards, blocked in gold.

A further and cheaper edition (203 × 146 mm.) with 8 monochrome half-tone plates and the same number of line drawings as the larger editions was also published. Bound in blue cloth-covered boards printed in black.

1910 *Collected Verse of Rudyard Kipling* illustrated by W. Heath Robinson. 392 pages, with 17 colour-plates and 12 line illustrations. 245 × 181 mm. Published by Doubleday, Page & Co., New York. Bound in red cloth-covered boards, blocked in gold.

There was no English edition of this handsome book.

1910 *The Dead King* by Rudyard Kipling illustrated by W. Heath Robinson. 48 pages, with 13 full-page borders and 10 other illustrations. 203 × 142 mm. Published by Hodder & Stoughton. Bound in purple cloth-covered boards and blocked in gold with a medallion of the head of Edward VII in the centre of the front board. Printed at the Edinburgh Press, London, on poor quality cream cartridge paper.

The illustrations consist of decorative borders on each page in a Morris-Gothic-Beardsley style. On some spreads there is only a small vignette appearing on the right hand page. These consist of an elongated heraldic motif topped by a crown, a lion or a unicorn.

A paper-back edition appeared at the same time.

1912 *Bill the Minder* written and illustrated by W. Heath Robinson. 256 pages with 16 tipped-in colour-plates and 126 line drawings. 242 × 184 mm. Published by Constable & Co., London. Bound in green cloth-covered boards blocked in gold with a four-colour illustration plate-sunk on the front board.

N.D. There was also a Limited Edition of 380 copies printed on hand-made paper and signed by the artist. 285 × 228 mm. Bound in white vellum and blocked in gold.

The original title for this book was *The King of Troy* but this was changed before publication. The illustration on the cover is a trimmed version of the frontispiece.

1913 *Hans Andersen's Fairy Tales* illustrated by W. Heath Robinson. 320 pages, with 16 tipped-in colour-plates and 93 line drawings. Published by Hodder & Stoughton. 248 × 191 mm. Bound in red cloth-covered boards, with white inlay panel on the front, blocked in gold.

A subsequent edition was produced for Boots the Chemists, poorly printed.

1917 Another later edition was produced in a smaller format 320 pages. 235 × 159 mm. by Hodder & Stoughton. This was bound in yellow cloth-covered boards, blocked in black and blue and with decorated endpapers.

N.D. There was also a Limited Edition of 100 copies printed on hand-made paper and signed by the artist. 292 × 225 mm. This was bound in white vellum and blocked in gold with a design of storks on the front board.

1914 *A Midsummer Night's Dream* by William Shakespeare, illustrated by W. Heath Robinson. 188 pages, with 12 tipped-in colour-plates, 32 full-page line drawings, decorated title-page and five other line half-title drawings. 279 × 219 mm. Published by Constable & Co., London. Bound in grey cloth-covered boards with a design of Titania blocked in gold and mauve foil over a printed design of a classical statue playing a flute and two fauns frolicking against a solid background of trees.

There was a cheaper edition, sold at 12/6d with a blue cloth cover printed only in black.

1914 There was also a Limited Edition of 250 copies 292 × 228 mm. and printed on hand-made paper and signed by the artist. An unspecified number were bound in white vellum covered boards and the remainder with green paper-covered boards and green cloth-covered spine, with a printed label.

1915 *The Water Babies* by Charles Kingsley illustrated by W. Heath Robinson. 320 pages, with 8 colour-plates, 52 full-page and 50 vignette line drawings. 213 × 165 mm. Published by Constable & Co., London. Bound in green cloth-covered boards blocked in gold.

1915 *Some Frightful War Pictures* by W. Heath Robinson. 48 pages, illustrated throughout with drawings that originally appeared in *The Sketch* and *The Illustrated Sporting and Dramatic News*. 138 × 210 mm. Published by Duckworth. Issued both in paper covers and in quarter-bound paper-covered boards with cloth backs and silhouette designs on the endpapers.

1916 Reprinted four times.

1916 *Hunlikely* by W. Heath Robinson, 56 pages, illustrated throughout. 252 × 187 mm. Published by Duckworth. Quarter-bound in buff paper-covered boards and a design on the front and a brown cloth spine. Decorated endpapers.

1916 *Peacock Pie* by Walter de la Mare. Illustrated by W. Heath Robinson. 180 pages, with a four-coloured frontispiece and 92 line drawings in the text and illustrated endpapers. 216 × 165 mm. Published by Constable & Co., London. Bound in green cloth-covered boards with a design on the front blocked in ivory and gold, gold-blocked spine.

1917 *The Saintly Hun: a book of German virtues* by W. Heath Robinson. 48 pages, illustrated by full-page line drawings. 337 × 213 mm. Paper cover. Published by Duckworth.

Many of these amusing drawings were in silhouette.

1918 *The Art of the Illustrator* by W. Heath Robinson. 16 pages with insets of the various stages of carrying out illustrations. 406 × 248 mm. Published by Percy V. Bradshaw. Paper covers.

1919 *Flypapers* by W. Heath Robinson. 64 pages, illustrated throughout. 305 × 213 mm. Saddle-stitched in paper-covered paper covers printed in blue and black. Published by Duckworth.

c. 1920 *Get On With It* by W. Heath Robinson. 56 page paperback with full-page line drawings. 295 × 213 mm. Published by G. Heath Robinson & J. Birch.

G. Heath Robinson was the only non-artist among the Robinson brothers.

1921 *The Home-Made Car* by W. Heath Robinson. 16 pages, with 5 full-page half-tone drawings and 13 line drawings. 279 × 216 mm. Published by Duckworth. Bound in an orange paper cover and priced 1/–.

1921 *Old-Time Stories* by Charles Perrault, translated by A. E. Johnson, illustrated by W. Heath Robinson. 200 pages, with 6 colour-plates 43 black-and-white illustrations and 6 uncaptioned vignettes. 251 × 178 mm. Published by Constable & Co. Ltd. Bound in red cloth-covered boards blocked in gold and with a roundel in gold and white let into the front board.

1962 A second edition.

1921 *Peter Quip in Search of a Friend*, written and illustrated by W. Heath Robinson. 8 chromo-lithographed plates and 17 line illustrations. Published by S. W. Partridge and printed by Thos. Foreman & Sons of Nottingham. Quarter-bound with green cloth spine and printed paper-covered boards. Illustrated endpapers.

This is a colourful book in the tradition of *The Child's Arabian Nights* (1903).

1922 *Quaint and Selected Pictures* by W. Heath Robinson. 16-pages illustrated with 13 sepia half-tone drawings. 318 × 222 mm. Published by G. Heath Robinson & J. Birch.

Many of these drawings had already appeared in *Get On With It*.

1923 *Humours of Golf* by W. Heath Robinson. 52 pages, 50 full-page illustrations and 6 vignettes. 277 × 216 mm. Bound in printed paper-covered boards. Published by Methuen & Co. Ltd.

There is a perspicacious and appreciative introduction by Bernard Darwin in which he says: 'His prodigal imagination always soars into more complicated regions . . . only a reader with a most comprehensive eye could get all his chuckling done at once.'

1923 *Topsy-Turvy Tales* by Elsie Smeaton, illustrated by W. Heath Robinson. 180 pages, with 6 colour plates and 35 black-and-white drawings. 210 × 168 mm. Published by John Lane, The Bodley Head. Printed by Butler & Tanner, Ltd., Frome, Somerset. Bound in blue cloth-covered boards, blocked with a design in black and orange.

1933 *The Incredible Adventures of Professor Branestawm* by Norman Hunter, illustrated by W. Heath Robinson with a coloured frontispiece, 66 black-and-white illustrations and illustrated endpapers. 204 pages. 210 × 165 mm. Published by John Lane. Bound in orange cloth-covered boards printed in dark blue.

1946 There was also a Penguin edition (178 × 108 mm.), with a drawn-on board cover printed in orange, yellow and black, and a further edition in 1965.

1934 *Absurdities: A Book of Collected Drawings* by Heath Robinson. 96 pages, 90 full-page drawings and 6 vignettes. 311 × 248 mm. Published by Hutchinson & Co. Ltd. Undated.

There were three editions of this book; an ordinary edition priced at 6/–; a de luxe edition at 12/6d; and a Limited Edition of 250 copies signed by the artist which sold at 25/–.

1934 *Balbus: a Latin reading book for junior forms* by G. M. Lyne, illustrated by Heath Robinson. 128 pages, with 12 line drawings. 175 × 118 mm. Published by Edward Arnold. Bound in blue cloth-covered boards blocked in gold.

1934 *Heath Robinson's Book of Goblins* from Vernaleken's *In the Land of Marvels*, 240 pages, with 7 colour-plates and 47 line illustrations. 242 × 178 mm. Published by Hutchinson & Co. Ltd. Bound in green imitation leather, blind blocked on the front and blocked in gold on the spine with rounded corners and gilded sides.

A second edition followed.

1936 *How to Live in a Flat* by K. R. G. Browne and Heath Robinson. 136 pages, illustrated throughout with line drawings. 184 × 96 mm. Published by Hutchinson & Co. Bound in orange cloth-covered boards, printed in black and with illustrated endpapers.

1937 *How to be a perfect Husband* by K. R. G. Browne and Heath Robinson. 130 pages, illustrated throughout with line drawings. 184 × 96 mm. Published by Hutchinson & Co. Bound in turquoise cloth-covered boards, blocked in black and with decorated endpapers.

1938 *How to Make a Garden Grow* by K. R. G. Browne and Heath Robinson. 112 pages, illustrated throughout with line drawings. 184 × 96 mm. Published by Hutchinson & Co. Bound in green cloth-covered boards blocked in black and with decorated endpapers.

1938 *My Line of Life* written and illustrated by W. Heath Robinson. 198 pages, with 15 half-tone plates and 115 line drawings. 248 × 184 mm. Published by Blackie & Sons. Bound in fawn cloth-covered boards printed in dark brown.

1930 *Success with Stocks and Shares* by John B. Gledhill and Frank Preston, illustrated by W. Heath Robinson. 135 pages with 4 line drawings. 210 × 140 mm. Published by Isaac Pitman & Sons. Bound in grey cloth-covered boards blocked in black.

1939 *How to be a Motorist* by K. R. G. Browne and Heath Robinson. 116 pages, illustrated throughout with line drawings. 184 × 96 mm. Published by Hutchinson & Co. Bound in red cloth-covered boards blocked in black and with decorated endpapers.

1939 *Let's Laugh* by K. R. G. Browne and Heath Robinson. 116 pages, illustrated throughout with line drawings. 184 × 96 mm. Published by Hutchinson & Co. Bound in yellow cloth-covered boards. Brown endpapers.

1940 *Mein Rant* by Richard F. Patterson. 80 pages, illustrated by W. Heath Robinson. with 13 line drawings, 194 × 134 mm. Published by Blackie. Bound in brown cloth-covered boards, blocked in dark brown.

1940 *How to Make the Best of Things* by H. Cecil Hunt and Heath Robinson. 128 pages, illustrated throughout with line drawings. 184 × 96 mm. Published by Hutchinson & Co. Bound in blue cloth-covered boards, blocked in black and with decorated endpapers.

1941 *How to Build a New World* by H. Cecil Hunt and W. Heath Robinson. 144 pages, illustrated throughout with line drawings. 84 × 121 mm. Published by Hutchinson & Co. Bound in blue cloth-covered boards blocked in black and with decorated endpapers.

1942 *Heath Robinson at War.* 48 pages, illustrated throughout with line drawings. 248 × 191 mm. Published by Methuen. Bound in green cloth-covered boards, printed in black with wrapper printed in black and yellow.

1943 *How to run a Communal Home*, by H. Cecil Hunt and W. Heath Robinson. 124 pages, illustrated throughout with line drawings. 184 × 121 mm. Published by Hutchinson & Co. Bound in red cloth-covered boards blocked in black, and with decorated endpapers.

1944 *Once upon a Time* by Liliane M. C. Clopet and illustrated by W. Heath Robinson. 108 pages, with 43 line drawings. 184 × 121 mm. Published by Frederick Müller. Bound in green cloth-covered boards, printed in black on the spine.

Booklets for Commerce and Advertising illustrated and sometimes written by W. Heath Robinson
This list is by no means complete. It is, however, an indication of the scope of the artist's work in this field. The best of these comic drawings are as good as any that Heath Robinson did for *The Sketch* or *The Bystander.*

Heath Robinson on Leather. Advertising booklet by W. Heath Robinson for Connolly Bros (Curriers) Ltd 311 × 248 mm. 48 pages illustrated in black and white. N.D.

Nothing takes the place of Leather. Advertising booklet by W. Heath Robinson for Connolly Bros (Curriers) Ltd. 140 × 216 mm. 20 pages with 18 line illustrations, in paper covers with an illustration printed in black and red. N.D.

Cattle Culture. Advertising booklet by W. Heath Robinson for Connolly Bros (Curriers) Ltd. 140 × 216 mm. 20 pages with 18 line illustrations, in paper covers with an illustration printed in green and black. N.D.

Connolly Chronicles retold by W. Heath Robinson. Advertising booklet for Connolly Bros (Curriers) Ltd. 273 × 197 mm. 20 pages with 22 line illustrations, in paper covers with illustrations printed in black and grey. 1933.

Connolly Land. Advertising booklet by W. Heath Robinson for Connolly Bros (Curriers) Ltd. 261 × 134 mm. 14 pages and fold-out 'Chart of Connolly Land', (242 × 388 mm.) 16 line and one four-colour illustration. In buff coloured paper covers, with a line illustration on the front cover printed in black. N.D.

Leather for Ever. Advertising booklet by W. Heath Robinson for Connolly Bros (Curriers) Ltd. 216 × 140 mm. 20 pages with 20 line illustrations, in cream coloured boards with an illustration printed in red and black.

This Coke Business. Cover design by W. Heath Robinson for an advertising booklet for Robert Cort & Sons Ltd, Reading. 219 × 214 mm. printed in brown and black on a cream coloured board showing an illustration of coke grading. N.D.

Behind the Scenes at Moss Bros with Heath Robinson. Advertising booklet 216×296 mm. 16 pages with 15 half-tone illustrations in board covers with an illustration printed in orange and black. N.D.

Then and Now. Advertising booklet illustrated by W. Heath Robinson for the Port of Manchester Warehouses Ltd. 283×219 mm. 48 pages with 6 half-tones and 16 line drawings, in brown paper covers with an illustration printed in black and yellow. 1921.

The Gentle Art of Excavating. Advertising booklet by W. Heath Robinson for Ruston-Bucyrus Ltd, Lincoln. 274×222 mm. 24 pages with 5 half-tone and 10 line drawings in buff coloured paper covers printed in brown. N.D.

The Gentle Art of Reproducing. Advertising booklet by W. Heath Robinson for the Practical Etching Service Ltd, London. Comments are by A. P. Garland. 305×238 mm. 28 pages and a fold-out four-colour illustration 'Prompt delivery' and 11 half-tone illustrations. In paper covers, with an illustration on the front printed in black, green and buff. 1931.

Advertising booklet by W. Heath Robinson for William Cooke and Co. Ltd (Makers of Wire Rope). 292×235 mm. 16 pages with 6 half-tone illustrations, in paper covers. N.D.

The Making of Asbestos Cement Roofings as seen by W. Heath Robinson. Advertising booklet for Asbestos Cement Building Products, London. 356×254 mm. 16 pages with 6 half-tone illustrations in grey board covers printed in black and blue, N.D.

Railway Ribaldry, a book by W. Heath Robinson celebrating the centenary of the Great Western Railway Company. 248×184 mm. 96 pages. Bound in drawn-on board covers with an illustration printed in green, yellow and black. Price 1/–. 1935.

In addition to numerous booklets, Heath Robinson illustrated several almanacks including:

The First Colliery for Fletcher Burrows and Co. Ltd, Atherton, Lancashire. 556×356 mm. with 4 half-tone drawings each 331×222 mm. 1923. These amusing drawings were very well printed by Tillotsons of Bolton.

The W. Heath Robinson Calendar for G. Delgardo Ltd, which contained a selection of comic drawings for this colour printer and publisher.

Books about Heath Robinson

1913 *The Book of W. Heath Robinson* by A. E. Johnson (In a series called Brush, Pen and Pencil). 52 pages with 6 colour plates, 8 half-tone, 16 full-page and line 31 vignette illustrations. 216×152 mm. Published by A. & C. Black. Bound in grey cloth-covered boards printed in black and blue.

A. E. Johnson was W. Heath Robinson's agent. He writes of Heath Robinson: '. . . I should portray Heath Robinson as a gentle amiable child, straying (with mouth and eyes wide open) through a world of commonplace wonders, admiringly observant of all about him – the odd shapes of trees, the whimsical cadence of the song of birds, the droll habits of perfectly respectable human persons – and vaguely conscious of a hidden significance in things which he does not attempt to probe. . . .'

1947 *The Life and Art of W. Heath Robinson* by Langston Day. 270 pages with 8 colour plates, 10 half-tone and 24 line illustrations. 216×140 mm. Published by Herbert Joseph. Bound in red cloth-covered boards, blocked in gold.

There is more about the 'life' than the 'art' in this study but there is a most interesting chapter on the relationship of Heath Robinson with his agent A. E. Johnson.

1966 *The Penguin Heath Robinson* with a foreword by R. Furneaux Jordan. 96 pages, illustrated throughout. 198×130 mm. Bound with a drawn-on board cover printed in black, cerise and orange.

This little book shows in 28 pages, illustrations from *Uncle Lubin, Bill the Minder, The Water Babies, A Midsummer Night's Dream, Peacock Pie* and *Old Time Stories.* The remainder of the book is devoted to the comic drawings.

Among numerous articles on Heath Robinson and his work, there is one in *The Sketch* of 4 January 1911 under the title of *A Most Inventive Humorist: Mr Heath Robinson.*

In *The Sketch* of 17 November 1915, his photograph appeared, surrounded by his own drawings as the first in a series of *Sketch* artists.

In *The Sunday Times Magazine* of 4 June 1972, an article entitled *Magic in his Madness* by Lesley Garner.

In *The Illustrated London News* of May 1972 an article entitled *Heath Robinson's Contraptions.*

Index

By the same author

Anatomy of Printing 1970
The Graphic Reproduction and Photography of Works of Art
  (with Edwin Smith) 1969
The Twentieth Century Book 1967
Illustration: Aspects and Directions (with Bob Gill) 1964
Typography: Basic Principles 1963
Printed Ephemera 1962
A Handbook of Type and Illustrations 1956
Graphic Design (with John Brinkley) 1954